THE GERMAN TRAVELMATE

compiled by
LEXUS
with
Ingrid Schumacher

D0525110

RICHARD DREW PUBLISHING
Glasgow

RICHARD DREW PUBLISHING LTD.
20 PARK CIRCUS
GLASGOW G3 6BE
SCOTLAND

First published 1982
First Reprint April 1982
Second Reprint May 1984
Third Reprint May 1985

ISBN 0 904002 90 X

Printed and bound in Great Britain by
Cox & Wyman Ltd.

YOUR TRAVELMATE
gives you one single easy-to-use list of useful
words and phrases to help you communicate in
German.

Built into this list are:
– Travel Tips with facts and figures which provide
  valuable information
– German words you'll see on signs and notices
– typical replies to some of the things you might
  want to say.

There is a menu reader on pages 72–73 and
numbers and the German alphabet are given on
the last page.

Your TRAVELMATE also tells you how to
pronounce German. Just read the pronunciations
as though they were English and you will
communicate – although you might not sound like
a native speaker.

There are some special sounds:
oo   is like oo in 'soon'
oo   is like oo in 'book'
$\overline{oo}$ is similar to the u sound in 'huge'
$\overline{o}$w   is like ow in 'cow'
k is like the ch in Scottish 'loch'

If no pronunciation is given then the word itself
can be spoken as though it were English. And
sometimes only part of a word or phrase needs a
pronunciation guide. Vowels given in italics show
which part of a word to stress.

a, an ein; eine; ein [ine; ine-uh]
  10 marks a litre zehn Mark der Liter
  [tsayn . . .]
aboard an Bord [bort]
Abfahrt departures
about: is he about? ist er da? [. . . air . . .]
  about 15 ungefähr fünfzehn [ᴔn-gheh-fair
  fōōnf-tsayn]
  at about 2 o'clock gegen zwei Uhr [gay-ghen
  tsvy oor]
above über [ōōber]
  above that darüber [da-rōōber]
abroad im Ausland [im ōws-lannt]
absolutely! genau! [gheh-nōw]
accelerator das Gas
accept annehmen [an-nay-men]
accident der Unfall [ōonfal]
  there's been an accident es ist ein Unfall
  passiert [. . . pas-ee-ert]
accommodation die Unterkunft [ᴔntèr-kᴔonft]
  we need accommodation for three wir
  brauchen Zimmer für drei [veer brōw-ken
  tsimmer fōōr dry]
» *TRAVEL TIP: as well as hotels there is the 'Hotel
  Garni' (bed and breakfast), 'Pension' (boarding
  house), 'Gasthof' (inn) or a room in a private
  house; look for the sign 'Zimmer frei' or
  'Fremdenzimmer'; information on local
  accommodation from railway station, look for
  'Zimmernachweis' or tourist information office*
accountant ein Wirtschaftsprüfer [veert-
  shaffts-prōōfer]
accurate genau [gheh-nōw]
ache der Schmerz [shmairts]
  my back aches ich habe Rückenschmerzen
  [ish hah-buh rōōcken-shmairtsen]

....

Achtung *caution, danger; (spoken) look out!*
(announcement) attention please

across über [ōober]; **how do we get across?**
wie kommen wir hinüber? [vee . . . veer]

ADAC Allgemeiner Deutscher Automobil-
Club *equivalent of AA, RAC*

adaptor der Zwischenstecker [tsvishen-sht–]

address die Adresse [ad-*r*essuh]
will you give me your address? würden Sie
mir Ihre Adresse geben? [vōorden zee meer
eeruh ad-ress-uh *g*ay-ben]

admission der Eintritt [ine–]

advance: in advance im voraus [im for-ōws]
can we book in advance? können wir im
voraus buchen? [*k*urrnen veer . . . boo-*k*en]

advert die Annonce [a-n*on*-suh]

afraid: I'm afraid I don't know das weiß ich
leider nicht [. . . vice ish ly-duh . . .]
I'm afraid so ja, leider
I'm afraid not leider nicht

after: after you nach Ihnen [nah*k* ee-nen]
after 2 o'clock nach zwei Uhr

afternoon der Nachmittag [nah*k*-mi-tahg]
in the afternoon nachmittags [–tahgs]
this afternoon heute nachmittag
[hoy-tuh . . .]
good afternoon guten Tag! [*g*oo-ten tahg]

aftershave das Rasierwasser [raz-*ee*r-vasser]

again wieder [veeder]

against gegen [*g*ay-ghen]

age das Alter [*a*l-ter]
under age minderjährig [m*i*nnder-yair-ri*k*]
it takes ages das dauert eine Ewigkeit [. . .
dowert ine-uh *a*y-vi*k*-kite]

agent der Vertreter [fair-tr*a*y-ter]

ago: a week ago vor einer Woche [for ine-uh
vock*uh*]
it wasn't long ago das ist noch nicht lange her
[dass isst no*k* nisht lang-uh hair]
how long ago was that? wie lange ist das
her? [vee . . .]

agree: I agree da stimme ich zu [. . . shtimmuh
ish tsoo]
  it doesn't agree with me das bekommt mir
  nicht [. . . buh-kommt meer nisht]
air die Luft [looft]
  by air per Flugzeug [pair floog-tsoyg]
  with air-conditioning mit Klimaanlage [. . .
  kleema-an-lahguh]
  by airmail per Luftpost [. . . looft-posst]
airport der Flughafen [floog-hah-fen]
alarm der Alarm
  alarm clock der Wecker [v–]
alcohol der Alkohol [–hohl]
  is it alcoholic? ist das Alkohol?
alive lebendig [lay-ben-dik]
  is he still alive? lebt er noch? [laybt air nok]
all: all the people alle Leute [al-uh loy-tuh]
  all night/all day die ganze Nacht/den ganzen
  Tag [dee gants-uh nahkt/dayn gants-en tahg]
  that's all wrong das ist ganz falsch
  all right! in Ordnung! [. . . ort-noong]
  that's all das ist alles [. . . al-ess]
  thank you – not at all danke – bitte [bittuh]
allergic: I'm allergic to . . . ich bin allergisch
gegen . . . [. . . al-air-ghish gay-ghen]
allowed erlaubt [air-lowpt]
  is it allowed? darf man das?
  it's not allowed das ist verboten! [fair-boh-
  ten]; **allow me** gestatten Sie mir
  [geh-shtat-ten zee meer]
almost fast [fasst]
alone allein [al-ine]
  did you come here alone? sind Sie allein
  hier? [zinnt zee . . . heer]
  leave me alone lassen Sie mich in Ruhe! [. . .
  zee mish in roo-uh]
Alps die Alpen
already schon [shohn]
also auch [owk]
alternator die Lichtmaschine [lisht-mash-ee-
nuh]

....

although obwohl [ob-v*oh*l]
altogether insgesamt [inz-gheh-z*a*mmt]
always immer
a.m. vormittags [f*o*r-mi-tahgs]
ambassador der Botschafter [b*o*ht-shaffter]
ambulance der Krankenwagen [kr*a*nken-
vah-ghen]
   get an ambulance! rufen Sie einen
   Krankenwagen! [r*oo*-fen zee ine-en . . .]
» *TRAVEL TIP: dial 110*
America Amerika [am-*ay*-ree-kah]
American amerik*a*nisch *(person)* Amerik*a*ner
(woman) Amerik*a*nerin
among unter [*oo*nter]
amp das Ampere [am-pair]
and und [*oo*nt]
angry böse [burr-zuh]
   I'm very angry about it ich bin deswegen
   sehr verärgert [. . . d*e*ss-vay-ghen zair fair-
   air-ghert]
   please don't get angry seien Sie bitte nicht
   böse! [zy-en zee bittuh . . .]
animal das Tier [teer]
ankle der (Fuß)knöchel [f*oo*ss-kuh-nurr-shell]
Ankunft arrivals
Anlieger frei residents only
Anmeldung reception
anniversary: it's our wedding anniversary
heute ist unser Hochzeitstag [hoy-tuh isst
*oo*n-ser h*oh*k-tsites-tahg]
annoy: he's annoying me er belästigt mich
[air bell-*e*st-i*k*t mish]
   it's very annoying das ist sehr ärgerlich [dass
   isst zair *air*-gherlish]
anorak der Anorak
another: can we have another room? können
wir ein anderes Zimmer haben? [k*u*rrnen veer
ine an-dress tsimmer h*a*h-ben]
   another beer, please noch ein Bier, bitte [n*o*k
   ine beer bittuh]
answer die Antwort [*a*nt-vort]

....

what was his answer? was hat er darauf
geantwortet? [vass hat air da-rōwf gheh-*a*nt-
vortet]

there was no answer *(tel)* es hat sich
niemand gemeldet [. . . zish n*ee*-mannt gheh–]

antifreeze der Frostschutz [–sh*oo*ts]

any: have you got any bananas/butter?
haben Sie Bananen/Butter? [h*a*h-ben zee ba-
nah-nen/b*oo*-ter]

I haven't got any ich habe keins [ish h*a*h-buh
kine-ts]

anybody (irgend) jemand [eer-ghent yay-
mannt]

can anybody help? kann jemand helfen?

anything (irgend)etwas [eer-ghent et-vass]

I don't want anything ich möchte gar nichts
[ish m*u*rrshtuh gahr nix]

aperitif ein Aperitif

apology eine Entschuldigung
[ent-sh*oo*l-dee-g*oo*ng]

please accept my apologies bitte, verzeihen
Sie mir [bittuh fair-ts*y*-en zee meer]

I want an apology ich warte auf eine
Entschuldigung [. . . vartuh ōwf ine-uh . . .]

appendicitis eine Blinddarmentzündung
[bl*i*nt-darm-ent-ts*ōō*n-d*oo*ng]

appetite der Appetit [–t*ee*t]

I've lost my appetite ich habe keinen Appetit
mehr [ish h*a*h-buh kine-en . . . mair]

apple ein Apfel

application form das Antragsformular
[–trahgs–]

appointment ein Termin [tair-m*ee*n]

can I make an appointment? könnte ich
einen Termin ausmachen? [k*u*rrntuh ish ine-
en . . . ōws-mah*k*en]

apricot eine Aprikose [app-ree-k*o*hzuh]

April April [appr*ee*l]

are sind [zinnt]

area die Gegend [g*a*y-ghent]

in the area in der Gegend

arm der Arm

around *see* **about**

arrange: will you arrange it? können Sie das
arrangieren? [ku̱rren zee dass ar-ron-djee-ren]
it's all arranged es ist alles arrangiert [ess
isst al-less ar-ron-djeert]

arrest verhaften [fair-ha̱ff-ten]
he's been arrested sie haben ihn verhaftet
[zee ha̱h-ben een . . .]

arrival die Ankunft [an-ko͞onft]

arrive ankommen
we only arrived yesterday wir sind erst
gestern angekommen [veer zinnt airst ghess-
tairn . . .]

art die Kunst [ko͞onst]
art gallery die Kunstgalerie

arthritis die Arthritis [ar-tree-tiss]

artificial künstlich [kö͞onstlish]

artist der Künstler [kö͞onstler]

as: as quickly as you can so schnell Sie
können [zoh shnell zee ku̱rren]
as much as you can so viel Sie können
[. . . feel . . .]
do as I do machen Sie es mir nach [mah̲ken
zee ess meer nah̲k]
as you like wie Sie wollen [vee zee vollen]

ashore an Land [an lannt]

ashtray ein Aschenbecher [a̲shen-beker]

ask fragen [fra̱h-ghen]
could you ask him to . . .? würden Sie ihn
bitten, ob er . . .? [vo͞orden zee een bit-en opp air]
that's not what I asked for das hab' ich nicht
bestellt [dass hahb ish nisht buh-shtellt]

asleep: he's still asleep er schläft noch [air
shlayft no̲k]

asparagus der Spargel [shpargel]

aspirin eine Kopfschmerztablette
[kopf-shmairts-tab-lettuh]

assistant der Assistent; *(in shop)* der Verkäufer
[fair-koy-fer]; *(woman)* die Assistentin; die
Verkäuferin

....

asthma das Asthma [asst-mah]
at: at the airport am Flughafen
  at my hotel in meinem Hotel
  at one o'clock um ein Uhr [oom ine oor]
atmosphere die Atmosphäre [–fay-ruh]
attitude die Einstellung [ine-shtell-oong]
attractive attraktiv [–teef]
  I think you're very attractive ich finde Sie
  sehr attraktiv [ish fin-duh zee zair . . .]
aubergine die Aubergine [–eenuh]
Aufzug lift
August August [ōw-goost]
aunt: my aunt meine Tante [mine-uh tantuh]
Ausfahrt exit (motorway)
Ausgang exit
Auskunft information
außer Betrieb out of order
Australia Australien [ōws-trah-lee-un]
Australian australisch [ōws-trah-lish]
  (person) Australier [–leer]
  (woman) Australierin
Austria Österreich [urr-ster-rysh]
Austrian österreichisch [–ish]; *(person)*
  Österreicher; *(woman)* Österreicherin
Ausverkauf sale
ausverkauft sold out
authorities die Behörden [buh-hurr-den]
automatic *(car)* der Automatik [ōw-toh-mah-
  tik]
autumn der Herbst [hairbst]
  in the autumn im Herbst
away: is it far away from here? ist es weit von
  hier? [isst ess vite fon heer]
  go away! geh (weg)! [gay vek]
awful schrecklich [–lish]
axle die Achse [ak-suh]
baby ein Baby
  we'd like a baby-sitter wir brauchen einen
  Babysitter [veer brōwken ine-en . . .]
back: I've got a bad back ich habe
  Schwierigkeiten mit meinem Rücken [ish

....

hah-buh shvee-ri*k*-kite-en mit mine-em
r̅o̅ocken]
I'll be back soon ich bin bald wieder da [ish
bin balt veeder dah]
is he back? ist er wieder da?
can I have my money back? kann ich mein
Geld wiederhaben [kan ish mine gellt
veeder-hah-ben]
come back kommen Sie zurück! [. . . zee
tsoo-r̅o̅ock]
I go back tomorrow ich fahre morgen zurück
[ish f*a*h-ruh mor-ghen . . .]
at the back hinten
bacon der Speck [shpeck]
bacon and eggs Eier mit Speck [eye-er . . .]
bad schlecht [shle*k*t]; **not bad** nicht schlecht
too bad Pech! [pe*k*]
Bad bathroom
Baden verboten no bathing
baggage das Gepäck [gheh-peck]
Bahnsteig platform
Bahnübergang level crossing
baker's der Bäcker [becker]
balcony der Balkon
a room with a balcony ein Zimmer mit
Balkon [ine tsimmer . . .]
ball der Ball [bal]
ball-point pen ein Kugelschreiber
[koogel-shryber]
banana eine Banane [bananuh]
band *(music)* die Band [bannt]
(dance) das Orchester [or*k*ester]
bandage die Binde [b*i*n-duh]
could you change the bandage? könnten
Sie den Verband wechseln? [k*u*rrnten zee dayn
fair-b*a*nnt ve*k*-seln]
bank die Bank
» *TRAVEL TIP: banking hours normally Mon-Fri
8.30–13.00 & 14.30–16.00 with late hours
Thursdays and sometimes Fridays closing
17.30; bank holidays see* **public**

bar die Bar

barber's der (Herren)friseur [(. . .)free-*zur*]

bargain: it's a real bargain das ist wirklich günstig [dass isst virk-lish *gōn*-sti*k*]

barmaid die Bardame [b*a*r-dah-muh]

barman der Barkeeper

basket der Korb [korp]

bath das Bad [baht]
can I have a bath? kann ich ein Bad nehmen? [kan ish ine baht n*a*y-men]
could you give me a bath towel? könnten Sie mir ein Badetuch geben? [k*u*rrnten zee meer ine b*a*h-duh-too*k* g*a*y-ben]

bathing costume der Badeanzug [b*a*h-duh-an-ts*oo*g]

bathroom das Badezimmer [b*a*h-duh-tsimmer]
we want a room with a private bathroom wir hätten gerne ein Zimmer mit Bad [veer hetten g*ai*rn-uh ine tsimmer mit baht]
can I use your bathroom? darf ich bitte mal Ihre Toilette benutzen? [darf ish bittuh mal ee-ruh twa-lettuh buh-n*oo*tsen]

battery die Batterie

be: to be sein [zine]
don't be angry seien Sie nicht böse [zy-en zee nisht burr-zuh]
be reasonable seien Sie vernünftig! [zy-en zee fair-n*ōō*nfti*k*]

beach der Strand [shtrannt]

beans die Bohnen [b*o*h-nen]

beautiful schön [shurrn]
that was a beautiful meal das Essen war ausgezeichnet [. . . var *ō*wss-gheh-tsyk*k*net]

because weil [vile]
because of the delay wegen der Verspätung [vayghen dair fair-sp*a*yt-*oo*ng]

bed ein Bett; **single bed/double bed** ein Einzelbett/Doppelbett [. . . ine-tsel-bett . . .]
you haven't changed my bed Sie haben die Bettwäsche nicht gewechselt [zee h*a*h-ben dee bett-vesh-uh nisht gheh-v*e*k-selt]

....

I'm off to bed ich geh'ins Bett [ish gay inz]
bed and breakfast Zimmer mit Frühstück
[tsimmer mit froo-shtoock]
bedroom das Schlafzimmer [shlahf-tsimmer]
bee eine Biene [bee-nuh]
beef das Rindfleisch [rinnt-flysh]
beer ein Bier [beer]
two beers, please zwei Bier, bitte [tsvy beer
bittuh]
YOU MAY THEN HEAR . . .
Pils oder Export *(Pils is stronger)*
große oder kleine *large or small (large = 0.5
litre, small = 0.2)*
eine Halbe = ½ litre = 0.9 pints
eine Maß *typical in Bavaria = 1 litre; if you like
a darker beer try 'ein Alt', though this is not
available in all parts of Germany*
before: before breakfast vor dem Frühstück
[for daym froo-shtoock]
before we leave bevor wir gehen [buh-for
veer gay-en]
I haven't been here before ich bin hier noch
nie gewesen [ish bin heer no*k* nee gheh-
v*a*y-zen]
begin: when does it begin? wann fängt es an?
[van fengt . . .]
beginner der Anfänger [*a*n-fenger]
behind hinter
Belgian belgisch [bel-ghish] *(person)* Belgier
[bel-gheer] *(woman)* Belgierin
Belgium Belgien [bel-ghee-un]
believe: I don't believe you das glaub' ich
Ihnen nicht [dass glowp ish ee-nen nisht]
I believe you ich glaub' Ihnen [ish glowp
ee-nen]
bell *(in hotel etc)* die Klingel
belong: that belongs to me das gehört mir
[dass gheh-hu*r*rt meer]
who does this belong to? wem gehört das?
[vaym gheh-hu*r*rt dass]
below unter [oonter]

belt der Gürtel [gōōrtel]

bend *(in road)* die Kurve [koor-vuh]

berries die Beeren [bay-ren]

berth *(on ship)* das Bett

besetzt *(toilet) engaged (bus) full*

beside neben [nay-ben]

best beste [best-uh]

    it's the best holiday I've ever had das ist der schönste Urlaub meines Lebens [. . . shurrn-stuh oor-lōwp mine-es lay-benz]

Betreten verboten *no trespassing*

Betreten des Rasens verboten *keep off the grass*

better besser

    haven't you got anything better? haben Sie nichts Besseres? [hah-ben zee nix . . .]

    are you feeling better? geht es Ihnen besser? [gayt ess ee-nen besser]

    I'm feeling a lot better es geht mir viel besser [ess gayt meer feel besser]

between zwischen [tsvishen]

bewachter Parkplatz *supervised car park*

beyond über [ōōber]

bicycle ein Fahrrad [fahr-raht]

big groß [grohss]

    a big one ein großer [ine grohss-er]

    that's too big das ist zu groß [. . . isst tsoo . . .]

    it's not big enough das ist nicht groß genug [dass isst nicht grohss gheh-noog]

    have you got a bigger one? haben Sie nichts Größeres? [hah-ben zee nix grurrss-er-es]

bikini ein Bikini

bill die Rechnung [resh-noong]

    could I have the bill, please? zahlen, bitte! [tsah-len bittuh]

binding *(ski)* die Bindung [–oong]

bird der Vogel [foh-ghel]

birthday der Geburtstag [gheh-boorts-tahg]

    it's my birthday ich habe Geburtstag

    happy birthday Herzlichen Glückwunsch (zum Geburtstag)! [hairts-lishen glōōck-voonsh tsoom gheh-boorts-tahg]

....

biscuit ein Keks
bit: just a bit nur ein bißchen [noor ine
 bis-shen]
 that's a bit too expensive das ist ein bißchen
 zu teuer [. . . bis-shen tsoo toy-er]
 just a little bit for me nur ganz wenig für
 mich [noor gants vay-nik foor mish]
 a bit of that cake ein Stückchen von dem
 Kuchen da [ine shtook-shen fon daim
 kooken . . .]
 a big bit ein großes Stück
bite ein Biß [biss]; *(mosquito)* ein Stich [stik]
bitte eintreten please enter
bitte klingeln please ring
bitte klopfen please knock
bitte nicht stören please do not disturb
bitter bitter; *(apple etc)* sauer [zow-er]
black schwarz [shvarts]
 he's had a blackout er ist ohnmächtig
 geworden [air isst ohn-mek-tik gheh-vorden]
blanket die Decke [deck-uh]
 I'd like another blanket könnte ich noch eine
 Decke haben? [kurrntuh ish nok ine-uh deck-uh
 hah-ben]
bleach das Bleichmittel [blysh–]
bleed bluten [blooten]
bless you *(after sneeze)* Gesundheit! [gheh-
 zoont-hyte]
blind blind [blinnt]; **blind spot** der tote
 Winkel [dair toh-tuh vinkel]
blister eine Blase [blah-zuh]
blocked *(pipe)* verstopft [fair-shtopft]
 (road) blockiert [block-eert]
blonde eine Blondine [blond-ee-nuh]
blood das Blut [bloot]
 his blood group is . . . er hat Blutgruppe . . .
 [air hat bloot-groop-uh . . .]
 I've got high blood pressure ich habe hohen
 Blutdruck [ish hah-buh hoh-en bloot-drook]
 he needs a blood transfusion er braucht
 eine Bluttransfusion [air browkt ine-uh

bloot-tranz-fooz-ee-ohn]
bloody mary eine Bloody Mary
blouse die Bluse [bloo-zuh]
blue blau [blōw]
board: full board Vollpension [foll penz-ee-ohn]; **half board** Halbpension [halp–]
boarding pass die Bordkarte [bort-kartuh]
boat das Boot [boht] *(bigger)* das Schiff [shiff]
boat train die Zugfähre [tsoog-fair-uh]
body der Körper [kurrper]
(dead body) eine Leiche [lysh-uh]
boil *(verb)* kochen [kok-en] *(med)* ein Furunkel [foor-oonkel]
boiled egg gekochtes Ei [gheh-koktes eye]
bone der Knochen [kuh-noken]
(fish) die Gräte [grayt-uh]
bonnet *(car)* die Motorhaube [–hōwbuh]
book das Buch [book]
booking office die Kasse [kassuh]
can I book a seat for …? kann ich einen Platz für … bestellen? [… fōr … buh-shtellen]
I'd like to book a table for two ich möchte gerne einen Tisch für zwei bestellen [ish murrshtuh gairn-uh ine-en tish fōr tsvy buh-shtellen]
bookshop eine Buchhandlung [book-hant-loong]
boot der Stiefel [shteefel]
(car) der Kofferraum [–rōwm]
booze der Alkohol
I had too much booze last night ich habe gestern abend zu viel getrunken [ish hah-buh ghestern ah-bent tsoo feel gheh-troonken]
border die Grenze [grents-uh]
» *TRAVEL TIP: visa and minimum of one night stay needed for crossing into GDR; transit visa can be bought at border for non-stop car journeys to West Berlin*
bored: I'm bored mir ist langweilig [meer isst lang-vile-ik]

boring langweilig [lang-vile-ik]

born: I was born in . . . ich bin in . . . geboren [ish bin in . . . geh-bor-ren] *see* **date**

boss der Chef

both beide [by-duh]

    I'll take both of them ich nehme beide [ish nay-muh by-duh]

bottle die Flasche [flash-uh]

    bottle-opener der Flaschenöffner [flash-en -urrfner]

bottom: at the bottom of the hill unten am Berg [oonten . . .]

bouncer der Rausschmeißer [rōwss-shmysser]

bowl *(basin)* die Schüssel [shōōssel]

box die Schachtel [shahktel] *(wood)* die Kiste [kistuh]

boy ein Junge [yoonguh]

boyfriend der Freund [froynt]

bra der BH [bay-hah]

bracelet das Armband [–bannt]

brake die Bremse [brem-zuh]

    could you check the brakes? könnten Sie die Bremsen nachsehen? [kurrnten zee dee brem-zen nahk-zay-en]

    I had to brake suddenly ich mußte plötzlich bremsen [ish moostuh plurrts-lish brem-zen]

    he didn't brake er hat nicht gebremst [air hat nisht gheh-bremst]

brandy der Weinbrand [vine-brannt]

bread das Brot [broht]

    could we have some bread and butter? könnten wir etwas Brot und Butter haben? [kurrnten veer etvass broht oont booter hah-ben]

    some more bread, please noch etwas Brot, bitte [nok etvass broht bittuh]

break brechen [breshen]

    I think I've broken my arm ich glaube, ich habe mir den Arm gebrochen [. . . glōwbuh ish hah-buh meer . . . gheh-broken]

breakdown die Panne [pan-uh]

I've had a breakdown mein Wagen ist
stehengeblieben [mine vah-ghen isst
shtay-en-gheh-bleeben]
nervous breakdown Nerven-
zusammenbruch [nairven-tsoo-zammen-br*oo*k]
» *TRAVEL TIP: motorway patrols give free help
(except parts); telephone for 'Straßenwachthilfe'*
[shtrahss-en-vah*k*t-hilfuh]
breakfast das Frühstück [fr*oo*-st*oo*ck]
English/Continental breakfast
englisches/kleines Frühstück
[. . . kline-es . . .]
breast die Brust [br*oo*st]
breath der Atem [ah-tem]
out of breath außer Atem [. . . *ō*wsser . . .]
breathe atmen [aht-men]
I can't breathe ich bekomme keine Luft [ish
buh-kommuh kine-uh l*oo*ft]
bridge die Brücke [br*ōō*ckuh]
briefcase die (Akten)mappe [(. . .)mappuh]
**brighten up: do you think it'll brighten up
later?** glauben Sie, es klärt sich später auf?
[gl*ō*wben zee es klairt zish spayter *ō*wf]
brilliant *(very good)* großartig [grohss-ahrti*k*]
bring bringen
could you bring it to my hotel? könnten Sie
es mir ins Hotel bringen? [kurrnten zee ess
meer ints . . .]
Britain Großbritannien [grohss-bri-t*a*hn-ee-un]
British britisch [br*ee*-tish]
the British die Briten [br*ee*-ten]
I'm British ich bin Brite; *(woman)* Britin
[br*ee*-tuh br*ee*-tin]
brochure der Prospekt
have you got any brochures about . . .?
haben Sie Prospekte über . . .? [h*a*h-ben zee . . .
*ōō*ber]
broken kaputt
you've broken it Sie haben es kaputt
gemacht [zee h*a*h-ben ess . . . gheh-mah*k*t]
my room/car has been broken into man hat

in mein Zimmer eingebrochen/man hat meinen
Wagen aufgebrochen [... mine tsimmer ine-
gheh-bro*k*en/... mine-en vah-ghen ōwf-gheh-
bro*k*en]

brooch die Brosche [broh-shuh]

brother: my brother mein Bruder [mine
brooder]

brown braun [brōwn]

brown paper das Packpapier [–pap*ee*r]

browse: can I just browse around? kann ich
mich mal umsehen? [kan ish mish mal oom-
zay-en]

bruise ein blauer Fleck [ine blōw-er ...]

brunette eine Brünette [ine-uh brōō-nettuh]

brush die Bürste [bōōrstuh] *(artist's)* der Pinsel

Brussels sprouts der Rosenkohl
[roh-zen-kohl]

bucket der Eimer [eye-mer]

buffet das Büffet [bōōf-ay] *(rail)* der
Speisewagen [shpyzuh-vah-ghen]

building das Gebäude [gheh-boy-duh]

bulb die (Glüh)birne [(glōō)beern-uh]

the bulb's gone die Birne ist durchgebrannt
[... isst dōorsh-gheh-brannt]

bump: he's had a bump on the head er hat
sich den Kopf angeschlagen [air hat zish dayn
kopf an-gheh-shlah-ghen]

bumper die Stoßstange [shtohss-shtang-uh]

bunch of flowers ein Blumenstrauß
[bl*oo*men-shtr*ō*wss]

bunk das Bett; *(in ship)* die Koje [koh-yuh]

bunk beds ein Etagenbett [ay-tahj-en–]

buoy die Boje [boh-yuh]

burglar ein Einbrecher [ine-bre*k*er]

they've taken all my money man hat mir
mein ganzes Geld gestohlen [... meer mine
ga*n*ts-es gelt gheh-shtohlen]

burnt: this meat is burnt das Fleisch ist
angebrannt [flysh isst an-gheh-brannt]

my arms are burnt ich habe Sonnenbrand an
den Armen [ish h*a*h-buh zonnen-brannt]

can you give me something for these burns? können Sie mir etwas für diese Brandwunden geben? [kurrnen zee meer etvass foor deez-uh brannt-voonden gay-ben]

bus der Bus [booss]

bus stop die Bushaltestelle [booss-haltuh-shtelluh]

could you tell me when we get there? können Sie mir sagen, wo ich aussteigen muß? [kurrnen zee meer zah-ghen voh ish owss-shty-ghen mooss]

» *TRAVEL TIP: bus travel; on town bus routes you may have to buy your ticket from a machine near the bus stop before you get on the bus*

business das Geschäft [gheh-sheft]

I'm here on business ich bin geschäftlich hier [ish bin gheh-sheft-lish heer]

business trip eine Geschäftsreise [ine-uh gheh-shefts-ry-zuh]

that's none of your business das geht Sie nichts an [dass gayt zee nix an]

bust die Büste [boostuh] *(measurement)* die Oberweite [ohber-vy-tuh]

(bankrupt) pleite [ply-tuh]

» *TRAVEL TIP: bust measurements*

UK	32	34	36	38	40
Germany	80	87	91	97	102

busy beschäftigt [buh-sheft-ikt]

(telephone) besetzt

are you busy? haben Sie viel zu tun? [hah-ben zee feel tsoo toon]

but aber [ah-ber]

not ... but ... nicht ... sondern ... [nisht ... zondern]

butcher's der Fleischer [flysher]

butter die Butter [booter]

button der Knopf [kuh-nopf]

buy kaufen [kowfen]

where can I buy ...? wo kann ich ... kaufen? [voh ...]

I'll buy it ich nehme es [ish nay-muh ess]

....

by: I'm here by myself ich bin allein hier [ish
bin al-ine heer]
  can you do it by tomorrow? können Sie es
  bis morgen erledigen? [ku*rr*en zee . . .
  air-la*y*d-i-ghen]
  by train/car/plane per Zug/Auto/Flugzeug
  [pair . . .]
  I parked by the trees ich habe bei den
  Bäumen geparkt [ish ha*h*-buh by dayn boy-men
  gheh-parkt]
  who's it made by? wer ist der
  Hersteller?[vair isst dair *hair*-shteller]
cabaret das Varieté [vah-ree-ay-ta*y*]
  (satire) das Kabarett [kabah-ra*y*]
cabbage der Kohl
cable das Kabel [ka*h*-bel]
cable-car die Seilbahn [zyle-bahn]
cabin *(on ship)* die Kabine [kab*ee*n-uh]
cafe ein Café
» *TRAVEL TIP: in the 'Konditorei' or 'Café' you will
  get mostly coffee and cakes; alcohol and snacks
  are served too; for a fuller café-type meal go to an
  'Imbißstube' or 'Schnellimbiß'; otherwise a pub*
cake der Kuchen [kook*en*]
  a piece of cake ein Stück Kuchen [ine sht*ōō*ck
  kook*en*]
calculator der Taschenrechner
  [tashen-reshner]
call: will you call the manager? rufen Sie den
  Geschäftsführer, bitte! [roofen zee dayn
  gheh-shefts-f*ōō*rer bittuh]
  what is this called? wie nennt man das?
  call box die Telefonzelle [–tselluh]
calm ruhig [roo-i*k*]
  calm down beruhigen Sie sich! [buh-roo-ig-en
  zee zish]
camera die Kamera
camp: can we camp here? können wir hier
  zelten? [ku*rr*en veer heer tselten]
  camping holiday ein Camping-Urlaub [. . .
  oor-lōwp]

campsite der Campingplatz
» *TRAVEL TIP: off-site camping requires permission of land-owner and/or local police*
can¹: a can of beer eine Dose Bier [ine-uh doh-zuh beer]
can-opener ein Dosenöffner [doh-zen-urrfner]
can²: can I have...? kann ich... haben? [kan ish... hah-ben]
can you...? können Sie... [kurrnen zee]
I can't... ich kann nicht... [ish kan nisht]
he can't... er kann nicht... [air...]
we can't... wir können nicht... [veer...]
Canada Kanada
Canadian kanadisch *(person)* Kanadier [kanah-deer] *(woman)* Kanadierin
cancel: I want to cancel my booking ich möchte meine Buchung rückgängig machen [ish murrshtuh mine-uh book-oong rōck-geng-ik mahken]
can we cancel dinner for tonight? können wir das Abendessen für heute abbestellen? [kurrnen veer das ah-bent-essen fōōr hoy-tuh app-buh-shtellen]
candle die Kerze [kairts-uh]
capsize kentern
car das Auto, der Wagen [ōw-toh, vah-ghen]
carafe die Karaffe [kar-affuh]
caravan der Wohnwagen [vohn-vah-ghen]
carburettor der Vergaser [fair-gahzer]
cards die Karten
do you play cards? spielen Sie Karten? [shpeelen zee...]
care: will you take care of my briefcase for me? würden Sie auf meine Aktenmappe aufpassen? [vōōrden zee ōwf mine-uh akten-mappuh ōwf-pas-en]
goodbye, take care mach's gut [mahks goot]
careful: be careful seien Sie vorsichtig [zy-en zee for-zik-tik]
car-ferry die Autofähre [ōw-toh-fair-uh]

car park der Parkplatz *(indoor)* das Parkhaus [park-hōwss]

carpet der Teppich [teppish]

carrot eine Karotte [karottuh]

carry: will you carry this for me? könnten Sie dies für mich nehmen? [kurrnten zee deess för mish nay-men]

  carry-cot die Baby-Tragetasche [baby-trah-gheh-tash-uh]

carving die Schnitzerei [shnits-er-*eye*]

case *(suitcase)* der Koffer

cash das Bargeld [b*a*r-gelt]

  I haven't any cash ich habe es nicht in bar [ish h*a*h-buh es nisht in b*a*r]

  cash desk die Kasse [k*a*ssuh]

  will you cash a cheque for me? können Sie mir einen Scheck einlösen? [kurrnen zee meer ine-en sheck *ine*-lurrzen]

casino das Kasino

castle das Schloß [schloss] *(fortress)* die Burg

cat eine Katze [kats-uh]

catch: where do we catch the bus? wo fährt der Bus ab? [voh fairt dair bōoss app]

  he's caught a bug er hat sich irgendwo angesteckt [air hat zish irgend-voh an-gheh-shteckt]

cathedral die Kathedrale [kah-tay-dr*a*hl-uh]

Catholic katholisch [kah-t*o*h-lish]

cauliflower der Blumenkohl [bloomen-kohl]

cave die Höhle [hurr-luh]

ceiling die Decke [d*e*ck-uh]

celery der Stangensellerie [shtang-en-zeller-ee]

cellophane das Cellophan [tsello-f*a*hn]

centigrade Celsius [tsel-zee-ooss]

» *TRAVEL TIP: to convert C to F:* $\frac{C}{5} \times 9 + 32 = F$

centigrade	-10	-5	0	10	15	21	30	36.9
Fahrenheit	14	23	32	50	59	70	86	98.4

centimetre ein Zentimeter [tsentee-may-ter]

» *TRAVEL TIP: 1 cm = 0.39 inches*

central zentral [tsen-trahl]

with central heating mit Zentralheizung
[mit tsen-trahl-hyts-oong]
centre das Zentrum [tsen-troom]
  how do we get to the centre? wie kommen
  wir zur Stadtmitte? [vee kommen veer tsoor
  shtatt-mittuh]
certain bestimmt [buh-shtimmt]
  are you certain? sind Sie sicher? [zint zee
  zisher]
certificate eine Bescheinigung
  [buh-shine-ee-goong]
chain die Kette [kettuh]
chair der Stuhl [shtool]
  (armchair) der Sessel [zessel]
chairlift der Sessellift
chambermaid das Zimmermädchen
  [tsimmer-mayd-shen]
champagne der Sekt [zekt]
change: could you change this into marks?
  könnten Sie das in Mark umtauschen?
  [kurrnten zee dass . . . oom-tow-shen]
  I haven't any change ich habe kein
  Kleingeld [ish hah-buh kine kline-gelt]
  do we have to change trains? müssen wir
  umsteigen? [moossen veer oom-shty-ghen]
  I'll have to get changed ich muß mich
  umziehen [ish mooss mish oom-tsee-en]
  I'd like to change my booking/flight etc ich
  möchte umbuchen [ish murrshtuh oom-booken]
channel: the Channel der Ärmelkanal
  [airmel-kanal]
charge: what do you charge? was verlangen
  Sie? [vass fair-langen zee]
  who's in charge? wer hat hier die Verant-
  wortung? [vair hat heer dee fair-ant-vort-oong]
chart *(flow chart etc)* das Diagramm
  [dee-ah-grahm]
cheap billig [billik]; **something cheaper**
  etwas Billigeres [etvass billig-er-es]
cheat: I've been cheated ich bin betrogen
  worden [ish bin buh-troh-ghen vorden]

....

check: will you check? sehen Sie bitte nach [zay-en zee bi*tt*uh nah*k*]

I've checked ich habe nachgeprüft [ish h*a*h-buh n*a*h*k*-gheh-pr�{oo}ft]

will you check the total? könnten Sie das nachrechnen? [k*u*rrnten zee das n*a*h*k*-resh-nen]

we checked in/we checked out wir haben uns angemeldet/abgemeldet [veer h*a*h-ben *oo*nts *a*ngheh-meldet/*a*pp-gheh-meldet]

cheek die Backe [b*a*ck-uh]

cheeky frech [fresh]

cheers Prost! [prohst]

(thank you) vielen Dank [feelen . . .]

cheerio Wiedersehen, Tschüs [veeder-zay-en, tsh\overline{oo}ss] *(toast)* Prost! [prohst]

cheese der Käse [k*a*y-zuh]

cheesecake der Käsekuchen [–koo*k*en]

say cheese bitte recht freundlich [bittuh re*k*t froynt-lish]

chef der Koch [ko*k*]

chemist's die Drogerie [drohgher-ee]

(dispensing) die Apotheke [apoh-t*a*y-kuh]

» *TRAVEL TIP: dispensing chemists display a notice about night service (Nachtdienst) and Sunday service (Sonntagsdienst)*

cheque der Scheck [sheck]

will you take a cheque? nehmen Sie Schecks? [nay-men zee shecks]

cheque book das Scheckbuch [sheck-book]

cheque card die Scheckkarte [sheck-kartuh]

chest die Brust [br*oo*st]

» *TRAVEL TIP: chest measurements*

UK	34	36	38	40	42	44	46
Germany	87	91	97	102	107	112	117

chewing gum der Kaugummi [k\overline{ow}-g*oo*mee]

chicken ein Hähnchen [hayn-shen]

chicken pox die Windpocken [vintpocken]

child ein Kind [kint]

children die Kinder [kinder]

children's portion ein Kinderteller

» *TRAVEL TIP: no law against taking children into a pub*

chin das Kinn

china das Porzellan [ports-ell*a*n]

chips die Pommes frites [pom freet] *(in casino)* die Chips

chocolate die Schokolade [shok-oh-l*a*hduh]
  hot chocolate (heiße) Schokolade [hyssuh]
  a box of chocolates Pralinen [prah-l*ee*nen]

choke *(car)* der Choke

chop ein Kotelett [kot-lett]
  pork/lamb chop Schweine-/Lammkotelett

Christian name der Vorname [for-nah-muh]

Christmas Weihnachten [vy-nah*k*-ten]
  happy Christmas fröhliche Weihnachten [frurrlish-uh . . .]
  Christmas Eve Heiligabend [hile-i*k*-ahbent]

» *TRAVEL TIP: Christmas in Germany starts on the 24th (Heiligabend) when work normally stops at midday; presents are given on the evening of the 24th; holidays on Christmas Day (der erste Weihnachtstag) and Boxing Day (der zweite Weihnachtstag); on December 6th children find sweets and nuts put in their shoes during the night by St Nikolaus*

church die Kirche [k*ee*r-shuh]
  where is the Protestant/Catholic church? wo ist die evangelische/katholische Kirche? [voh ist dee . . .] ,

cider der Apfelmost

cigar die Zigarre [tsig*a*rruh]

cigarette die Zigarette [tsig*a*rr-ettuh]
  would you like a cigarette? darf ich Ihnen eine Zigarette anbieten? [. . . ish een-en ine-uh tsigarr-ettuh an-bee-ten]

» *TRAVEL TIP: don't be offended if you're not offered a cigarette; normally everybody smokes their own*

cine-camera die Filmkamera

cinema das Kino [k*ee*-noh]

circle der Kreis [krice]

....

city die Stadt [shtatt]

claim *(insurance)* der Anspruch [an-shprook]

clarify klären [klairen]

clean *(adjective)* sauber [zowber]
   can I have some clean sheets? kann ich
   frische Bettwäsche haben? [kann ish frish-uh
   bett-vesh-uh hah-ben]
   my room hasn't been cleaned today in
   meinem Zimmer ist heute nicht saubergemacht
   worden [in mine-em tsimmer isst hoy-tuh nisht
   zowber-gheh-mahkt vorden]
   it's not clean das ist nicht sauber

cleansing cream die Reinigungscreme
   [rine-ee-goongs-kray-muh]

clear klar
   I'm not clear about it ich bin mir darüber
   nicht im klaren [ish bin meer daröober
   nisht . . .]

clever klug [kloog] *(skilful)* geschickt
   [gheh-shickt]

climate das Klima [klee-mah]

climb: we're going to climb . . . wir
   besteigen . . . [veer buh-shty-ghen]
   climber ein Bergsteiger [bairk-shty-gher]
   climbing boots die Bergstiefel [–shteefel]

clip *(ski: on boot)* die Schnalle [shnall-uh]

cloakroom die Garderobe [garduh-robe-uh]
   (WC) die Toilette [twa-lettuh]

clock die Uhr [oor]

close¹: nahe [nah-uh]
   (weather) schwül [shvool]

close²: when do you close? wann machen Sie
   zu? [van mahken zee tsoo]

closed geschlossen [gheh-shlossen]

cloth das Tuch [took]

clothes die Kleider [kly-der]
   clothes peg die Wäscheklammer [vesh-uh–]

cloud die Wolke [vol-kuh]

clutch die Kupplung [koop-loong]
   the clutch is slipping die Kupplung schleift
   [. . . shlyft]

coach der (Reise)bus [(ry-zuh)booss]
  coach party die Reisegesellschaft
  [ry-zuh-gheh-zell-shafft]
coast die Küste [koostuh]
  coastguard die Küstenwache
  [koosten-vah*k*-uh]
coat der Mantel
cockroach eine Küchenschabe
  [koo*k*en-shah-buh]
coffee ein Kaffee [*k*affay]
  white coffee/black coffee Kaffee mit
  Milch/Kaffee schwarz [. . . mit milsh/
  . . . shvarts]
  two coffees, please zwei Kaffee, bitte [tsvy
  kaffay bittuh]
  YOU MAY THEN HEAR . . .
  Kännchen oder Tassen? *pots or cups?* [ken-shen
  oh-der . . .] *a pot is usually 2 cups; coffee and
  cream are always served separately*
coin die Münze [moon-tsuh]
cold kalt
  I'm cold ich friere [ish free-ruh]
  I've got a cold ich bin erkältet [ish bin
  air-*k*eltet]
collapse: he's collapsed er ist zusammen-
  gebrochen [air isst tsoo-za*mm*en-gheh-bro*k*en]
collar der Kragen [*k*rah-ghen]
  collarbone das Schlüsselbein [shloossel-bine]
» *TRAVEL TIP: continental sizes*

(old) UK:	14	14½	15	15½	16	16½	17
continental:	36	37	38	39	41	42	43

collect abholen [app-hoh-len]
  can I collect my shirts? ich möchte meine
  Hemden abholen [ish m*u*rrshtuh m*i*ne-uh . . .]
collision der Zusammenstoß
  [tsoo-za*mm*en-shtohss]
colour die Farbe [*f*ar-buh]
  have you any other colours? haben Sie noch
  andere Farben? [h*a*h-ben zee no*k* ander-uh
  far-ben]
comb ein Kamm

come kommen
   I come from London ich komme aus London
[ish kommuh ōwss . . .]
   we came here yesterday wir sind gestern
hier angekommen [veer zint ghestern heer
*a*n-gheh-kommen]
   when is he coming? wann kommt er? [van
kommt air]
   come on! komm!
   come with me kommen Sie mit! [. . . zee . . .]
comfortable bequem [buh-kv*a*ym]
   it's not very comfortable es ist nicht sehr
bequem [. . . nisht zayr buh-kv*a*ym]
Common Market die EWG [ay-vay-gay]
communication cord die Notbremse
[note-brem-zuh]
company die Gesellschaft [gheh-z*e*ll-shafft]
   you're good company ich bin gern mit Ihnen
zusammen [ish bin gairn mit ee-nen
tsoo-zammen]
compartment *(train)* das Abteil [app-tile]
compass der Kompaß [kom-pas]
compensation die Entschädigung
[ent-sh*a*yd-ee-g*oo*ng]
   I demand compensation ich verlange
Schadenersatz [ish fair-l*a*ng-uh
sh*a*den-airsats]
complain sich beschweren [zish buh-shv*a*iren]
   I want to complain about the waiter ich
möchte mich über den Kellner beschweren [ish
m*u*rrshtuh mish ōōber dayn kellner . . .]
   have you got a complaints book? das
Beschwerdebuch, bitte!
[dass buh-shvair-duh-b*oo*k bittuh]
completely völlig [furrl*i*k]
complicated: it's very complicated es ist sehr
kompliziert [. . . zair komplits-eert]
compliment das Kompliment [–ment]
   my compliments to the chef mein Lob der
Küche
[mine lohp dair kōōk-uh]

concert das Konzert [kontsairt]

concussion eine Gehirnerschütterung [gheh-hirn-air-shoot-eroong]

condition die Bedingung [buh-ding-oong]
  it's not in very good condition es ist nicht in besonders gutem Zustand [... nisht in buh-zonders gootem tsoo-shtant]

conference die Konferenz [kon-fer-ents]

confession das Geständnis [gheh-shtent-nis]

confirm bestätigen [buh-stayt-ee-goong]

confuse: you're confusing me Sie bringen mich durcheinander [zee bringen mish doorsh-ine-ander]

congratulations! herzlichen Glückwunsch! [hairts-lishen glöck-voonsh]

conjunctivitis die Bindehautentzündung [binduh-howt-ent-tsöon-doong]

con-man der Schwindler [shvintler]

connection die Verbindung [fair-bin-doong]

connoisseur der Kenner [kenner]

conscious bewußt [buh-voosst]

consciousness: he's lost consciousness er ist bewußtlos [air ist buh-vosst-lohs]

constipation die Verstopfung [fair-shtopf-oong]

consul der Konsul [kon-zool]

consulate das Konsulat [kon-zool-aht]

contact: how can I contact . . .? wie kann ich . . . erreichen? [vee kann ish . . . air-ryshen]
  I'll get in contact soon ich werde mich melden [ish vairduh mish . . .]
  contact lenses die Kontaktlinsen [–zen]

contraceptive ein empfängnisverhütendes Mittel [emp-feng-nis-fair-höot-end-ess . . .]

convenient günstig [goonstik]

cook: it's not cooked es ist nicht gar
  it was beautifully cooked das war vorzüglich [dass var for-tsöog-lish]
  you're a good cook Sie kochen ausgezeichnet [zee koken öwss-gheh-tsyk-net]

cooker der Herd [hairt]

cool kühl [kool]

....

corkscrew der Korkenzieher [–tsee-er]
corn *(foot)* ein Hühnerauge [hōōner-ōwg-uh]
corner die Ecke [eck-uh]
  can we have a corner table? können wir
  einen Ecktisch haben? [kʊrrnen veer ine-en
  eck-tish hah-ben]
cornflakes die Cornflakes
correct richtig [rik-tik]
cosmetics die Kosmetika [kosmaytikah]
cost: what does it cost? was kostet das? [vass
  kostet dass]
  that's too much das ist zu viel [dass isst tsoo
  feel]
  I'll take it ich nehme es [ish nay-muh ess]
cotton die Baumwolle [bōwm-volluh]
  cotton wool die Watte [vattuh]
couchette der Liegesitz [leeg-uh-zits]
cough der Husten [hoosten]
  cough drops die Hustentropfen
  cough mixture der Hustensaft [–zaft]
could: could you please... könnten Sie, bitte,
  ...? [kʊrrnten zee bittuh ...]
  could I have...? dürfte ich ... haben?
  [dōōrf-tuh ish ... hah-ben]
  we couldn't... wir konnten nicht ... [veer]
country das Land [lannt]
  in the country auf dem Land [ōwf daym lannt]
couple: a couple of... ein paar ... [ine pahr]
courier der Reiseleiter [ry-zuh-ly-ter]
course *(of meal)* der Gang
  of course natürlich [natōōr-lish]
court: I'll take you to court ich werde Sie vor
  Gericht bringen [ish vair-duh zee for gheh-rikt
  ...]
cousin der Cousin; die Cousine [koo-zan
  koo-zeen-uh]
cover: keep him covered decken Sie ihn zu
  [... zee een tsoo]
  cover charge ein Gedeck [gheh-deck]
cow die Kuh [koo]
crab die Krabbe [krabbuh]

....

crash: there's been a crash da ist ein Unfall
passiert [da isst ine oon-fal pas-eert]
  crash helmet der Sturzhelm [shtoorts-helm]
crazy verrückt [fair-rookt]
  you're crazy du spinnst [doo shpinnst]
cream die Sahne [zah-nuh] *(with butter)* die
Creme [kray-muh]
  (for skin) die Creme
  (colour) cremefarben [–far-ben]
creche die Kinderkrippe [kinder-krippuh]
credit card die Kreditkarte [kredeet-kartuh]
crisis die Krise [kree-zuh]
crisps die Chips
cross roads die Kreuzung [kroytsoong]
crowded überfüllt [oober-foolt]
cruise die Bootsfahrt [bohts-fahrt]
crutch die Krücke [krook-uh]
cry: don't cry weinen Sie nicht [vine-en zee
nisht]
cup die Tasse [tass-uh]; **a cup of coffee** eine
Tasse Kaffee [ine-uh tass-uh kaffay]
cupboard der Schrank [shrank]
curry der Curry
curtains der Vorhang [for-hang]
cushion das Kissen
Customs der Zoll [tsoll]
cut: I've cut myself ich habe mich geschnitten
[ish hah-buh mish gheh-shnitten]
cycle: can we cycle there? können wir mit
dem Rad dorthin fahren? [kurrnen veer mit
daym raht dort-hin far-ren]
  cyclist der Radfahrer [raht-far-rer]
cylinder der Zylinder [tsoolinder]
  cylinder head gasket die Zylinderkopf-
dichtung [tsoolinder-kopf-dik-toong]
dad(dy) der Papa
damage: I'll pay for the damage ich werde für
den Schaden aufkommen [ish vair-duh foor
dayn shahden oowf-kommen]
  it's damaged es ist beschädigt [es isst
buh-shayd-ikt]

....

Damen *Ladies*

damn! verdammt! [fair-da̲mmt]

damp feucht [foysht]

dance: is there a dance on? ist da Tanz?
   would you like to dance? möchten Sie
   tanzen? [mu̲rrshten zee tantsen]

dangerous gefährlich [geh-fa̲ir-lish]

dark dunkel [do̲onkel]
   when does it get dark? wann wird es dunkel?
   [van virt ess do̲onkel]
   dark blue dunkelblau [do̲onkel-blō̲w]

darling Liebling [leep-ling]

dashboard das Armaturenbrett [–tooren–]

date: what's the date der wievielte ist heute?
   [dair vee-fe̲el-tuh isst ho̲y-tuh]
   can we fix a date? können wir einen Termin
   abmachen? [ku̲rrnen veer ine-en tair-me̲en
   app-mahk̲en]
   on the fifth of May am fünften Mai [am
   fo̲onften my]
   in 1951 neunzehnhunderteinundfünfzig
   [noyn-tsayn-ho̲ondert-ine-o̲ont-fo̲onf-tsik̲]

» *TRAVEL TIP: to say the date in German add letters*
   'ten' to the number if 1–19, and 'sten' if 20–31;
   see numbers on p 128; exceptions: **first** ersten;
   third dritten; **seventh** siebten

daughter: my daughter meine Tochter
   [mine-uh tok̲ter]

day der Tag [tahg]

dazzle: his lights were dazzling me seine
   Scheinwerfer haben mich geblendet [zine-uh
   shine-vairfer hah-ben mish gheh– . . .]

Deutsche Demokratische Republik, DDR *GDR*

dead tot [toht]

deaf taub [tō̲wp]

deal *(business)* das Geschäft [geh-sheft]
   it's a deal abgemacht [app-gheh-mahk̲t]
   will you deal with it? kümmern Sie sich,
   bitte, darum? [ko̲om-ern zee zish bittuh
   da-ro̲om]

dear *(expensive)* teuer [toyer]

Dear Mr Kunz Sehr geehrter Herr Kunz
Dear Franz Lieber Franz
Dear Sir *if no name known write:* Sehr geehrte
Damen und Herren
December Dezember [dayts–]
deck das Deck
  deckchair der Liegestuhl [leeguh-shtool]
declare: nothing to declare nichts zu
verzollen [nix tsoo fair-tsollen]
deep tief [teef]
defendant der Angeklagte [an-gheh-klahg-tuh]
(in civil cases) der Beklagte [buh–]
de-icer der Enteiser [ent-eyes-er]
delay: the flight was delayed der Flug hatte
Verspätung [dair floog hat-uh fair-shpayt-oong]
deliberately absichtlich [app-zisht-lish]
delicate *(person)* zart [tsart]
delicatessen ein Delikatessengeschäft
[–gheh-sheft]
delicious köstlich [kurrst-lish]
delivery die Lieferung [leeferoong]
  is there another mail delivery? gibt es noch
eine Zustellung? [gheept ess nok ine-uh
tsoo-shtel-oong]
de luxe Luxus– [looxooss]
democratic demokratisch [–krah-tish]
demonstration *(of gadget)* eine Vorführung
[for-főor-roong]
dent die Delle [delluh]
  you've dented my car Sie haben mir mein
Auto eingedellt [zee hah-ben meer mineőw-toh
ine-gheh-dellt]
dentist der Zahnarzt [tsahn-artst]
  YOU MAY HEAR ...
  bitte weit öffnen *open wide*
  bitte ausspülen *rinse out*
dentures das Gebiß [gheh-biss] *(partial)* die
Zahnprothese [tsahn-proh-tay-zuh]
deny: I deny it das bestreite ich [dass
buh-shtry-tuh ish]
deodorant das Deodorant [day–]

departure die Abreise [app-ry-zuh]
(bus, train) die Abfahrt
(plane) der Abflug [app-floog]
depend: it depends das kommt darauf an [. . .
da-rōwf . . .]
it depends on him das kommt auf ihn an
deport deportieren [–ee-ren]
deposit die Anzahlung [antsah-lœng]
do I have to leave a deposit? muß ich eine
Kaution hinterlegen? [mœss ish ine-uh
kōw-tsee-ohn hinterlay-ghen]
depressed deprimiert [day-prim-*ee*rt]
depth die Tiefe [teefuh]
desperate: I'm desperate for a drink ich
brauche dringend was zu trinken [ish brōw*k*uh
dringent . . . tsoo . . .]
dessert der Nachtisch [nah*k*–]
destination das Reiseziel [ry-zuh-tseel]
(of goods) der Bestimmungsort
[buh-shtim-œngs-ort]
detergent das Waschmittel
detour der Umweg [œm-vegg]
devalued abgewertet [*a*pp-gheh-vairtet]
develop: could you develop these? könnten
Sie diese entwickeln? [k*u*rrnten zee dee-zuh
ent-v––]
diabetic ein Diabetiker [dee–] *(woman)* eine
Diabetikerin
(adjective) diabetisch [dee-ah-bay-tish]
dialling code die Vorwahl [for-vahl]
diamond der Diamant [dee–]
diarrhoea der Durchfall [dœrsh-fal]
**have you got something for
diarrhoea?** haben Sie ein Mittel gegen
Durchfall? [h*a*h-ben zee . . .]
diary das Tagebuch [t*a*h-gheh-boo*k*]
dictionary ein Wörterbuch [v*u*rr-ter-boo*k*]
die sterben [shtairben]
he's dying er stirbt [air shteerbt]
diesel *(fuel)* Diesel
diet die Diät [dee-ayt]

I'm on a diet ich mache eine Schlankheitskur [ish mah*k*-uh ine-uh shlank-hites-koor]

different: they are different sie sind verschieden [zee zint fair-sh*ee*-den]
  can I have a different room? kann ich ein anderes Zimmer haben? [. . . ine an-der-es . . .]
  is there a different route? gibt es eine andere Strecke?

difficult schwierig [shveeri*k*]

digestion die Verdauung [fair-d*ow*-*oo*ng]

dinghy das Ding(h)i; *(collapsible)* das Schlauchboot [shl*ow*k-boht]

dining room das Eßzimmer [ess-tsimmer] *(in hotel)* der Speiseraum [shpy-zuh-r*ow*m]

dinner *(evening)* das (Abend)essen [ah-bent–] *(lunch)* das (Mittag)essen [mittahg]
  dinner jacket die Smokingjacke [–yackuh]

dipped headlights Abblendlicht [app-blent-lisht]

direct *(adjective)* direkt [dee–]
  does it go direct? ist es eine Direkt-verbindung? [ine-uh deerekt-fairbind*oo*ng]

dirty schmutzig [shm*oo*tsik]

disabled behindert [buh-h*i*nndert]

disappear verschwinden [fair-shv*i*nnden]
  it's just disappeared es ist einfach verschwunden [ess isst ine-fah*k* fair-shv*oo*nden]

disappointing enttäuschend [ent-toyshent]

disco die Disko

discount der Rabatt
  cash discount Skonto

disgusting widerlich [veeder-lish]

dish *(food)* das Gericht [gheh-r*i*sht] *(plate)* die Schüssel [sh*oo*ssel]

dishonest unehrlich [*oo*n-airlish]

disinfectant das Desinfektionsmittel [days-infek-tsee-*o*hns–]

dispensing chemist's die Apotheke [–taykuh]

distance die Entfernung [ent-f*ai*r-n*oo*ng]
  in the distance in der Ferne [in dair fairnuh]

....

distress signal ein Notsignal [noht-zignahl]

distributor *(car)* der Verteiler [fair-tyler]

disturb: the noise is disturbing us der Lärm
stört uns [dair lairm shturrt oonz]

divorced geschieden [gheh-sh*ee*den]

do machen [mah*k*en]

    how do you do? guten Tag [gooten tahg]

    what are you doing tonight? was machen
Sie heute abend? [vass . . . zee hoytuh ah-bent]

    how do you do it? wie machen Sie das?
[vee . . . zee . . .]

    will you do it for me? machen Sie das für
mich? [. . . f*oo*r mish]

    I've never done it before ich habe das noch
nie gemacht [ish h*a*h-buh dass no*k* nee
gheh-mah*k*t]

    I was doing 60 kph ich fuhr mit 60 km/h [ish
foor mit ze*k*-tsi*k*]

doctor der Arzt

    I need a doctor ich brauche einen Arzt [ish
br*ow*kuh ine-en . . .]

    YOU MAY HEAR...

    haben Sie das schon einmal gehabt? *have you
had this before?*

    wo tut es weh? *where does it hurt?*

    nehmen Sie zur Zeit Medikamente? *are you
taking any drugs at the moment?*

    nehmen Sie eine davon dreimal/viermal täglich
take one of these three/four times a day

document das Dokument [–ooment]

dog ein Hund [h*oo*nt]

don't! nicht! [nisht] *see* **not**

door die Tür [t*oo*r]

dosage die Dosis [doh-ziss]

double: double room Doppelzimmer
[–tsimmer]

    double whisky ein doppelter Whisky

down: get down! runter! [r*oo*nter]

    it's down the road es ist nur ein Stückchen
weiter [. . . noor ine sht*oo*k-shen vy-ter]

    he's downstairs er ist unten [. . . *oo*nten]

drain das (Abfluß)rohr [app-flooss-ror]

drawing pin die Reißzwecke [rice-tsvecker]

dress das Kleid [klite]

» *TRAVEL TIP: dress sizes*

UK	10	12	14	16	18	20
Germany	38	40	42	44	46	48

  dressing gown der Bademantel [bah-duh–]

  dressing *(for wound)* der Verband [fair-bannt]
  (for salad) die Sauce [zohsuh]

drink: would you like a drink? möchten Sie
etwas trinken? [murrshten zee etvass . . .]

  I don't drink ich trinke keinen Alkohol [ish
trinkuh kine-en al-koh-hohl]

  is the water drinkable? kann man das
Wasser trinken?

» *TRAVEL TIP: licensing hours far less strict in
Germany; drinks can be served at all hours*

drive fahren

  I've been driving all day ich bin den ganzen
Tag gefahren [ish . . . gantsen tahg gheh–]

driver der Fahrer

driving license der Führerschein [foorer-shine]

» *TRAVEL TIP: driving in Germany; speed limits: 50
kph (31 mph) in town; 100 (62) outside;
motorways 130 (81) recommended with 60 (37)
minimum; trucks and caravans max. 80 (49);
driving on side lights illegal; seat belt, red
triangle and first aid kit compulsory*

drown: he's drowning er ertrinkt [air
airtrinkt]

drücken push

drug das Medikament; *(cannabis etc)* die Droge
[droh-ghuh]

drunk *(adjective)* betrunken [buh-troonken]

dry trocken

  dry-clean chemisch reinigen [shaymish
ry-niggen]

due: when is the bus due? wann soll der Bus
ankommen? [van zoll dair booss . . .]

Durchfahrt verboten no through road

Durchgangsverkehr through traffic

....

during während [vair-rent]

Duschen showers

dust der Staub [shtōwp]

Dutch holländisch [hol-ɛnd-ish]

   Dutchman Holländer

   Dutchwoman Holländerin

duty-free *(noun)* das Duty-free

dynamo der Dynamo [dōn-ahmoh]

each: can we have one each? können wir jeder eins haben? [kurrnen veer yay-der ine-ts hah-ben]

   how much are they each? was kosten sie pro Stück? [vass kosten zee proh shtōōk]

ear das Ohr [or]

   I have earache ich habe Ohrenschmerzen [ish hah-buh or-ren-shmairtsen]

early früh [frōō]

   we want to leave a day earlier wir möchten einen Tag früher abreisen [veer murrshten ine-en tahg frōō-uh app-ry-zen]

earring der Ohrring [or-ring]

east der Osten

Easter Ostern [oh-stern]

easy leicht [lysht]

eat essen; **something to eat** etwas zu essen [ett-vass tsoo . . .]

egg ein Ei [eye]

Einbahnstraße one-way street

Einfahrt (to) motorway

Eingang entrance

einordnen get in lane

Einstieg vorn/hinten enter at the front/rear

Eintritt frei admission free

Eire Irland [eer-lannt]

either: either . . . or . . . entweder . . . oder [ɛnt-vay-der oh-der]

   I don't like either mir gefällt beides nicht [meer gheh-fɛllt by-des nisht]

elastic elastisch

   elastic band ein Gummiband [gōōmee-bannt]

elbow der Ellbogen [el-boh-ghen]

electric elektrisch
  electric blanket eine Heizdecke
  [h*i*tes-deckuh]
  electric fire ein elektrisches Heizgerät
  [. . . h*i*tes-gheh-rayt]
electrician der Elektriker
electricity die Elektrizität [elek-trits-i-t*a*yt]
elegant elegant [el-ay-g*a*nnt]
else: something else etwas anderes
  [ett-vass . . .]
  somewhere else irgendwo anders
  [eer-ghent-voh . . .]
  let's go somewhere else gehen wir woanders
  hin! [gay-en veer vo . . .]
  who else? wer sonst? [vair . . .]
  or else sonst
embarrassing peinlich [pine-lish]
embarrassed verlegen [fair-l*a*y-ghen]
embassy die Botschaft [boht-shafft]
emergency der Notfall [noht-fal]
empty leer [layr]
enclose: I enclose . . . ich lege . . . bei
end das Ende; **when does it end?** bis wann
  geht es? [biss van gayt ess]
engaged *(telephone, toilet)* besetzt [buh-z*e*tst]
  (person) verlobt [fair-lohbt]
engagement ring der Verlobungsring
engine die Maschine [mash-*ee*-nuh] *(of car,*
  plane) der Motor [moh-t*o*r]
  engine trouble Schwierigkeiten mit dem
  Motor [shvee-ri*k*-kite-en mit daym . . .]
England England [eng-glannt]
English englisch
  the English die Engländer [eng-glender]
  I'm English ich bin Engländer
  (woman) ich bin Engländerin
enjoy: I enjoyed it very much ich habe es sehr
  genossen [ish h*a*h-buh ess zair gheh—]
  enjoy yourself viel Spaß! [feel shpass]
  I enjoy riding/driving ich reite/fahre gern
  [ish ry-tuh/f*a*h-ruh gairn]

....

enlargement *(photo)* die Vergrößerung [fair-grurrs-eroong]

enormous enorm [ay-norm]

enough genug [gheh-noog]

    thank you, that's enough danke, das reicht [dankuh dass rysht]

entertainment die Unterhaltung [oonter-halt-oong]

entrance der Eingang [ine-gang]

entry der Eintritt [ine–]

    entry permit *(for GDR)* der Passierschein [pas-eer-shine]

envelope ein Umschlag [oom-shlahg]

equipment die Ausrüstung [ōws-rōōst-oong]

    electrical equipment Elektrogeräte [–gheh-rayt-uh]

Erdgeschoß ground floor

Erfrischungen refreshments

error der Fehler [fayler]

erste Hilfe first aid

Erwachsene adults

escalator die Rolltreppe [–puh]

especially besonders [buh-zonnders]

essential notwendig [noht-ven-dik]

    it is essential that ... es ist unbedingt erforderlich, daß ... [ess isst oon-buh-dingt air-ford-uh-lish dass]

Europe Europa [oy-roh-pa]

evacuate evakuieren [ay-vak-oo-ee-ren]

even: even the British sogar die Briten [zoh-gar dee bree-ten]

evening der Abend [ah-bent]

    good evening guten Abend [gooten ...]

    this evening heute abend [hoytuh ...]

evening dress der Abendanzug [–an-tsoog] *(woman's)* das Abendkleid [–klite]

ever: have you ever been to ...? sind Sie jemals in ... gewesen? [zinnt zee yay-malz in ... gheh-vay-zen]

every jeder [yay-duh]

    every day jeden Tag [yay-den tahg]

everyone jeder
  is everyone ready? sind alle fertig? [zinnt al-uh fair-ti*k*]
  everything alles [al-less]
  everywhere überall [ōōber-al]
evidence der Beweis [buh-vice]
exact(ly) genau [gheh-nōw]
example das Beispiel [by-shpeel]
  for example zum Beispiel [tsoom . . .]
excellent ausgezeichnet [ōwss-gheh-tsysh-net]
except: except me außer mir [ōwss-uh meer]
excess: excess baggage Übergewicht [ōōber-gheh-visht]
  excess fare die Nachlösegebühr [nah*k*-lurr-zuh-gheh-bōōr]
exchange *(money)* die Wechselstube [vek-sel-shtoo-buh]
  (telephone) das Fernamt [fairn-amt]
exciting aufregend [ōwf-ray-ghent]
excursion der Ausflug [ōwss-floog]
  excursion ticket verbilligte Fahrkarte [fair-bill-i*k*tuh fahr-kartuh]
excuse: excuse me entschuldigen Sie! [ent-shool-dig-en zee]
exhaust *(car)* der Auspuff [ōwss-poof]
exhausted erschöpft [air-shupft]
exhibition die Ausstellung [ōwss-shtel-ōong]
exhibitor der Aussteller [ōwss-shteller]
exit der Ausgang [ōwss-gang]
expect erwarten [air-varten]
  she's expecting sie ist in anderen Umständen [zee isst in an-duh-ren oom-shtenden]
expenses die Kosten
  it's on expenses das geht auf Spesen [dass gayt ōwf shpay-zen]
expensive teuer [toy-er]
expert der Experte [–pair-tuh]
explain erklären [air-klairen]
  would you explain that slowly? könnten Sie das langsam erklären? [ku rrnten zee dass . . .]
export *(noun)* der Export

....

exposure meter der Belichtungsmesser [buh-lishtœngs–]
express *(send letter)* per Expreß [pair express]
extra zusätzlich [tsoo-zets-lish]
  an extra glass/day ein Glas/Tag extra [ine glahss/tahg ex-trah]
  is that extra? wird das extra berechnet? [veert dass . . . buh-resh-net]
extremely äußerst [oyss–]
eye das Auge [ōw-guh]
  eyebrow die Augenbraue [ōw-ghen-brōw-uh]
  eyeshadow der Lidschatten [leet-shat-en]
  eye witness der Augenzeuge [–tsoy-guh]
face das Gesicht [gheh-zisht]
fact die Tatsache [taht-zahk-uh]
factory die Fabrik [fab-reek]
Fahrenheit Fahrenheit

» *TRAVEL TIP: to convert F to C:* $F - 32 \times \frac{5}{9} = C$

Fahrenheit	14	23	32	50	59	70	86	98.4
centigrade	−10	−5	0	10	15	21	30	36.9

Fahrkarten tickets
faint: she's fainted sie ist ohnmächtig geworden [zee isst ohn-mesh-tik gheh-vorden]
fair *(fun—)* der Jahrmarkt [yah–]
  (commercial) die Messe [mess-uh]
  that's not fair das ist nicht fair
faithfully: yours faithfully hochachtungsvoll
fake *(noun)* eine Fälschung [fell-shoong]
fall fallen [fal-en]
  he's fallen er ist gefallen [air isst gheh–]
false falsch
family die Familie [fam-ee-lee-uh]
fan der Ventilator [–ah-tor]
  (football etc) der Fan [fen]
fan belt der Keilriemen [kile-ree-men]
far weit [vite]
  is it far? ist es weit? [isst ess vite]
  how far is it? wie weit ist es? [vee . . .]
fare *(travel)* der Fahrpreis [fahr-price]
  (on plane) der Flugpreis [floog-price]

....

farm der Bauernhof [bōw-ern-hohf]
farther weiter [vy–]
fashion die Mode [moh-duh]
fast schnell
   don't speak so fast sprechen Sie nicht so
   schnell! [shpreshen zee nisht zoh . . .]
fat dick *(noun)* das Fett
fatally tödlich [turrt-lish]
father: my father mein Vater [mine fah–]
fault der Fehler [fayler]
   it's not my fault das ist nicht meine Schuld
   [dass isst nisht mine-uh shoolt]
faulty defekt [dayfekt]
favourite *(adjective)* Lieblings– [leep-lings]
   my favourite city meine Lieblingsstadt
   [mine-uh leep-lings-shtatt]
February Februar [fay-broo-ar]
fed-up: I'm fed-up ich habe die Nase voll [ish
   hah-buh dee nah-zuh foll]
feel: I feel cold/hot/sad mir ist kalt/heiß/ich
   bin irgendwie traurig [meer isst kalt/hice/ish
   bin eer-ghent-vee trōw-rik]
   I feel like . . . ich habe Lust auf . . . [ish
   hah-buh loost ōwf]
Feierabend! *we're closing*
Fernsprecher *telephone*
ferry die Fähre [fay-ruh]
fetch: will you come and fetch me? werden
   Sie mich abholen? [vairden zee mich
   app-hoh-len]
Feuermelder *fire alarm*
fever das Fieber [feeber]
few wenige [vay-nig-uh]
   only a few nur ein paar [noor ine pahr]
   a few days ein paar Tage [ine pahr tah-guh]
fiancé: my fiancé mein Verlobter [mine
   fair-lohb-ter]
fiancée: my fiancée meine Verlobte [mine-uh
   fair-lohb-tuh]
fiddle: it's a fiddle das ist Schiebung [dass isst
   shee-boong]

....

field das Feld [fellt] *(grass)* die Wiese [vee-zuh]

fifty-fifty fifty-fifty

figure die Zahl [tsahl]

   (of person) die Figur [fig-oor]

   I'm watching my figure ich muß auf meine Figur achten [ish mooss ōwf mine-uh . . . ahk-ten]

fill füllen [fool-en]

   fill her up volltanken, bitte [foll– bittuh]

   to fill in a form ein Formular ausfüllen [. . . ōws-fool-en]

fillet das Filet [feelay]

filling *(tooth)* eine Plombe [plom-buh]

film der Film

   do you have this type of film? haben Sie solche Filme? [hah-ben zee zolshuh . . .]

filter *(traffic)* die Abbiegerspur [app-bee-gher-spoor]

   filter or non-filter? mit Filter oder ohne? [. . . oh-der oh-nuh]

find finden [finn-den]; **if you find it . . .** wenn Sie es finden . . . [ven zee ess . . .]

   I've found a . . . ich habe ein . . . gefunden [ish hah-buh ine . . . gheh-foonden]

fine: fine weather schönes Wetter [shurrn-ess v–]

   a 50 marks fine eine Geldbuße von fünfzig Mark [ine-uh ghellt-boo-zuh fon foonf-tsik . . .]

   OK, that's fine das ist gut [dass isst goot]

finger der Finger [finng-uh]

fingernail der Fingernagel [–nah-ghel]

finish: I haven't finished ich bin noch nicht fertig [ish bin nok nisht fair-tik]

fire: fire! Feuer! [foy-uh]

   can we light a fire here? können wir hier ein Feuer anzünden? [kurrnen veer heer ine . . . an-tsoonden]

   it's not firing *(car)* es zündet nicht [ess tsoondet nisht]

   fire extinguisher der Feuerlöscher [–lurrscher]

fire brigade die Feuerwehr [–vair]
» *TRAVEL TIP: dial 112*
firm *(noun)* die Firma [feer-mah]
first erste [air-stuh]
  I was first ich war erster [ish var . . .]
  first aid Erste Hilfe [. . . hill-fuh]
  first aid kit der Verbandskasten
  [fair-bannts–]
  first class erste Klasse [. . . klass-uh]
  first name der Vorname [for-nah-muh]
fish der Fisch
fishing das Angeln [ang-eln]
  fishing rod/tackle die Angelrute/das
  Angelzeug [ang-el-rootuh/–tsoyg]
fix: can you fix it? *(arrange, repair)* können Sie
  das machen? [kurrnen zee dass mahken]
fizzy mit Kohlensäure [mit kohlen-zoy-ruh]
flag die Fahne [fah-nuh]; *(national, ship's)* die
  Flagge [flag-uh]
flash *(phot)* das Blitzlicht [–likt]
flat flach [flahk]
  this drink is flat das schmeckt abgestanden
  [dass . . . app-gheh-shtanden]
  I've got a flat (tyre) ich habe einen Platten
  [ish hah-buh ine-en . . .]
  (apartment) die Wohnung [voh-nong]
flavour der Geschmack [gheh–]
flea der Floh
flies der Reißverschluß [rice-fair-shlooss]
flight der Flug [floog]
flirt *(verb)* flirten
float schwimmen [shvimmen]
floor der Boden [boh-den]
  on the second floor im zweiten Stock
  [. . . tsvy-ten shtock]
flower die Blume [bloo-muh]
flu die Grippe [grip-uh]
fly *(insect)* die Fliege [flee-guh]
foggy neblig [nay-blik]
follow folgen [foll-ghen]
  follow me folgen Sie mir [. . . zee meer]

....

food das Essen; *(groceries)* die Lebensmittel [lay-benz–]
  food poisoning Lebensmittelvergiftung [–fair-ghif-toong]
  see pages 72–73
fool der Narr
foot der Fuß [fooss]
  » *TRAVEL TIP: 1 foot = 30.1 cm = 0.3 metres*
football Fußball [fooss-bal]
for für [foor]
forbidden verboten [fair-boh-ten]
foreign ausländisch [ōws-lend-ish]
  foreign exchange Devisen [day-vee-zen]
foreigner ein Ausländer [ōws-lender]
forest der Wald [valt]
forget vergessen [fair-ghessen]
  I forget, I've forgotten ich habe es vergessen [ish hah-buh ess . . .]
  don't forget vergessen Sie nicht [. . . zee nisht]
  I'll never forget you ich werde dich nie vergessen [. . . vair-duh dish nee . . .]
fork die Gabel [gah-bel]
form *(document)* das Formular [form-oo-lar]
formal formell; *(person, manner)* förmlich [furrm-lish]
fortnight vierzehn Tage [feer-tsayn tah-guh]
forward *(adverb)* vorwärts [for-vairtz]
  forwarding address die Nachsendeadresse [nahk-zenduh-ad-ressuh]
  could you forward my mail? könnten Sie mir die Post nachsenden? [kurrnten zee meer dee posst nahk-zenden]
foundation cream die Grundierungscreme [groon-deer-roongs-kray-muh]
fracture der Bruch [brook]
fragile zerbrechlich [tsair-brek-lish]
France Frankreich [–rysh]
fraud der Betrug [buh-troog]
free frei [fry]
  admission free Eintritt frei [ine–]

frei *(toilet)* vacant *(taxi)* free
Freibad *open-air pool*
freight die Fracht [frah*k*t]
Fremdenzimmer *rooms*
French französisch [frants-*u*rr-zish]
   (person) Franzose [frants-oh-zuh]
   (woman) Französin [frants-*u*rrs-zin]
freshen up: I want to freshen up ich möchte
   mich frischmachen [ish m*u*rrshtuh mish
   fr*i*sh-mah*k*-en]
Friday Freitag [fry-tahg]
fridge der Kühlschrank [k$\overline{oo}$l–]
friend ein Freund [froynt]
friendly freundlich [froynt-lish]
from von [fon]
   from England aus England [$\overline{o}$wss eng-glannt]
   where is it from? wo kommt es her?
   [voh . . . ess hair]
front *(noun)* die Vorderseite [for-der-zy-tuh]
   in front of you vor Ihnen [for ee-nen]
   in the front vorn [forn]
frost der Frost
   frostbite die Frostbeule [–boy-luh]
frozen *(food)* tiefgekühlt [t*e*ef-gheh-k$\overline{oo}$lt]
   (person) eiskalt [ice–]
fruit das Obst [ohpst]
   fruit salad der Obstsalat [*o*hpst-zal-*a*ht]
fry braten [br*a*h-ten]
   nothing fried nichts Gebratenes [nix
   gheh-br*a*h-ten-ess]
   fried egg ein Spiegelei [shp*e*e-ghel-eye]
   frying pan die Bratpfanne [br*a*ht-pfann-uh]
full voll [foll]
fun: it's fun das macht Spaß [dass mah*k*t
   shpass]
Fundbüro *lost property*
funny *(strange, comical)* komisch [k*o*h–]
furniture die Möbel [m*u*rr-bel]
further weiter [vy–]
fuse die Sicherung [zisher-*oo*ng]
fuss das Theater [tay-*a*h-ter]

....

future die Zukunft [tsoo-koonft]
gale der Sturm [shtoorm]
gallon die Gallone [gal-oh-nuh]
» *TRAVEL TIP: 1 gallon = 4.55 litres*
gallstone ein Gallenstein [gal-en-shtine]
gamble spielen [shpee-len]; *(on horses)* wetten [vet-en]
gammon der Vorderschinken [for-duh-shinken]
garage *(repair)* die Werkstatt [vairk-shtatt]
  (petrol) die Tankstelle [–shtel-uh]
  (parking) die Garage [ga-rah-djuh]
garden der Garten
garlic der Knoblauch [kuh-nohp-lowk]
gas das Gas; *(petrol)* das Benzin [ben-tseen]
  gas cylinder der Gaszylinder [–tsoo-linnder]
gasket die Dichtung [disht-toong]
gay *(homosexual)* schwul [shvool]
gear der Gang
  (equipment) die Ausrüstung [ows-rōos-toong]
  gearbox trouble Getriebeschaden
  [gheh-tree-buh-shah-den]
  gear lever der Schaltknüppel [–kuh-nōō-pel]
  (column-mounted) der Schalthebel [–hay-bel]
  I can't get it into gear ich kann den Gang
  nicht einlegen [ish kann dayn . . . nisht
  ine-lay-ghen]
Gebühren charges
Gefahr danger
Gegenverkehr oncoming traffic
gents die Herrentoilette [heh-ren-twah-lettuh]
geöffnet open
Gepäckaufbewahrung left luggage
German deutsch [doytsh]; *(person)* Deutscher
  (woman) Deutsche [doytsh-uh]
  I don't speak German ich spreche kein
  Deutsch [ish shpresh-uh kine doytsh]
  the Germans die Deutschen
Germany Deutschland [doytsh-lannt]
geschlossen closed
Geschwindigkeitsbegrenzung speed limit
gesture eine Geste [ghay-stuh]

get: will you get me a . . .? holen Sie mir bitte
ein . . .? [hoh-len zee meer bittuh ine]
   how do I get to? wie komme ich zu . . .? [vee
komm-uh ish tsoo]
   when can I get it back? wann bekomme ich
es zurück? [van buh-komm-uh ish ess tsoo-rōōk]
   where do I get off? wo muß ich aussteigen?
[voh mooss ish ōwss-shty-ghen]
   when do we get back? wann sind wir zurück?
[van zinnt veer tsoo-rōōk]
   where do I get a bus for . . .? wo fährt der Bus
nach . . .? [voh fairt dair booss nahk . . . app]
   have you got . . .? haben Sie . . .? [hah-ben
zee]
gin ein Gin
   gin and tonic ein Gin Tonic
girl ein Mädchen [mayd-shen]
   my girlfriend meine Freundin [mine-uh
froyn-din]
give geben [gay-ben]
   I gave it to him ich habe es ihm gegeben [ish
hah-buh ess eem gheh-gay-ben]
glad froh
glandular fever das Drüsenfieber [–zen-feeber]
glass das Glas
   a glass of water ein Glas Wasser [vasser]
glasses die Brille [brill-uh]
Glatteis *black ice*
Gleis *platform*
gloves die Handschuhe [hannt-shoo-uh]
glue der Klebstoff [klayp-shtoff]
GmbH *Gesellschaft mit beschränkter Haftung*
Ltd
go gehen [gay-en] *(by vehicle)* fahren
   where are you going? wo gehen Sie hin?
   my car won't go mein Auto fährt nicht [mine
ōw-toh fairt nisht]
   when does the bus go? wann fährt der Bus?
[vann fairt dair booss]
   he's/it's gone er/es ist weg
[air/ess isst vek]

can I have a go? kann ich es versuchen?
[kann ish ess fair-*zoo-k*en]
goal das Tor
goat die Ziege [ts*ee*-guh]
god Gott
goggles *(ski)* die Schneebrille [shnay-brill-uh]
gold das Gold [gollt]
golf Golf
good gut [goot]
goodbye auf Wiedersehen [ōwf vee-duh-zayn]
gooseberries Stachelbeeren [sht*ak*-el-bay-ren]
gramme ein Gramm
» *TRAVEL TIP: 100 grammes = approx 3½ oz*
grand großartig [grohss-art*ik*]
  my grandfather mein Großvater [–fah–]
  my grandmother meine Großmutter
  [–m*oo*t–]
  my grandson mein Enkel
  my granddaughter meine Enkelin
  [eng-kel-inn]
grapes Trauben [trōw-ben]
  grapefruit die Grapefruit
  grapefruit juice ein Grapefruitsaft [–zafft]
grass das Gras
grateful dankbar
  I'm very grateful to you ich bin Ihnen sehr
  dankbar [ish bin ee-nen zair . . .]
gratitude die Dankbarkeit [–kite]
gravy die Soße [z*oh*-suh]
grease das Fett; *(car etc)* die Wagenschmiere
  [v*a*h-ghen-shmee-ruh]
greasy fettig [–i*k*]
great groß; *(very good)* großartig [–arti*k*]
  great! klasse! [klass-uh]
greedy gierig [gh*ee*-ri*k*]
green grün [grōōn]
  green card die grüne Karte [. . . kart-uh]
  greengrocer's der Obst– und Gemüsehändler
  [ohbst oont geh-mōō-zuh-hentler]
grey grau [grōw]
grocer's der Kaufmann [kōwf–]

ground der Boden [boh-den]
  on the ground auf dem Boden [owf daym . . .]
  on the ground floor im Erdgeschoß [. . .
  airt-gheh-shoss]
group die Gruppe [groop-uh]
  our group leader der Leiter unserer Gruppe
  [ly-ter oon-zuh-ruh . . .]
  I'm with the English group ich gehöre zur
  englischen Gruppe [ish gheh-hurr-uh tsoor
  eng-glish-en . . .]
guarantee die Garantie
  is there a guarantee? bekommen wir eine
  Garantie? [buh-kommen veer ine-uh . . .]
guest der Gast
guesthouse die Pension [pen-zee-ohn]
guide der Führer [fooruh]
guilty schuldig [shool-dik]
guitar die Gitarre [ghee-ta-ruh]
gum *(in mouth)* der Gaumen [gow-men]
gun das Gewehr [gheh-vair]
  (pistol) die Pistole [–oh-luh]
gynaecologist der Gynäkologe
  [goo-nay-koh-loh-guh]
hair das Haar
  hairbrush die Haarbürste [–boor-stuh]
  where can I get a haircut? wo kann ich mir
  die Haare schneiden lassen? [voh kann ish meer
  dee hah-ruh shnyden lassen]
  is there a hairdresser's here? gibt es hier
  einen Friseur? [gheept ess heer ine-en
  free-zurr]
  hair grip die Haarklemme [–klem-uh]
» *TRAVEL TIP: hairdressers close on Mondays*
half halb [halp]
  a half portion eine halbe Portion [hal-buh
  portsee-ohn] **half an hour** eine halbe Stunde
  [. . . shtoon-duh]
halt stop
ham der Schinken
  hamburger ein Hamburger
hammer ein Hammer

....

hand die Hand [hannt]
   handbag die Handtasche [–tash-uh]
   handbrake die Handbremse [–brem-zuh]
handkerchief das Taschentuch [tash-en-took]
handle der Griff
hand luggage das Handgepäck [–gheh-peck]
handmade handgearbeitet
  [hannt-gheh-ar-by-tet]
handsome gutaussehend [goot-ōws-zay-ent]
hanger der Kleiderbügel [kly-duh-bōō-gel]
hangover der Kater [kahter]
  my head is killing me mir platzt fast der Kopf
  [meer . . . fasst dair . . .]
happen geschehen [gheh-shay-en]
  I don't know how it happened ich weiß
  nicht, wie es geschehen ist [ish vice nisht vee
  ess . . .]
  what's happening/happened? was ist los?
  [vass isst lohs]
happy glücklich [glōōk-lish]
harbour der Hafen [hah-fen]
hard hart; *(difficult)* schwierig [shvee-rik]
  hard-boiled egg ein hartgekochtes Ei
  [–gheh-kok-tes eye]
  push hard fest drücken [. . . drōōken]
harm der Schaden [shah-den]
hat der Hut [hoot] *(knitted)* die Mütze [mōōt-suh]
hate: I hate . . . ich hasse . . . [ish hass-uh]
have haben [hah-ben]
  I have no time ich habe keine Zeit [ish
  hah-buh kine-uh tsite]
  do you have any cigars/a map? haben Sie
  Zigarren/eine Karte? [hah-ben zee . . .]
  can I have some water/some more? kann
  ich etwas Wasser/noch ein bißchen haben?
  [kann ish ett-vass vasser/nok ine biss-shen
  hah-ben]
  I have to leave tomorrow ich muß morgen
  abreisen [ish mooss mor-ghen app-ry-zen]
hayfever der Heuschnupfen [hoy-shnoop-fen]
Hbf Hauptbahnhof central station

he er [air] **he is** er ist
head der Kopf
  headache Kopfschmerzen [–schmair-tsen]
  headlight der Scheinwerfer [shine-vairfer]
  head waiter der Oberkellner [ohber–]
health die Gesundheit [gheh-zoont-hite]
  your health! auf Ihr Wohl! [owf eer vohl]
healthy gesund [gheh-zoont]
hear: I can't hear ich höre nichts [ish hurr-uh
  nix]
  hearing aid das Hörgerät [hurr-gheh-rayt]
heart das Herz [hairts]
  heart attack ein Herzinfarkt
heat die Hitze [hit-suh]
  heat stroke ein Hitzschlag [hits-shlahg]
heating die Heizung [hites-oong]
heavy schwer [shvair]
heel der Absatz [app-zats]
  could you put new heels on these? könnten
  Sie neue Absätze darauf machen? [kurrnten zee
  noy-uh app-zets-uh dah-rowf mahken]
height die Höhe [hurr-uh]
  (person's) die Größe [grurr-suh]
heiß hot
hello hallo
help helfen
  can you help me? würden Sie mir helfen?
  [voorden zee meer . . .]
  help! Hilfe! [hill-fuh]
her sie [zee]
  will you give it to her? würden Sie es ihr
  geben? [voorden zee ess eer gay-ben]
  it's her bag, it's hers es ist ihre Tasche, es ist
  ihre [ess isst ee-ruh tash-uh]
here hier [heer]
  come here komm her! [. . . hair]
Herren gents
high hoch [hohk]
hill der Berg [bairk]
  up/down the hill den Berg hinauf/hinunter
  [dayn . . . hin-owf/hin-oonter]

....

him ihn [een]
   will you give it to him? würden Sie es ihm
   geben? [vōōrden zee ess eem gay-ben]
   it's him er ist es [air isst ess]
hire *see* **rent**
his sein [zine]
   it's his drink, it's his es ist sein Drink, es ist
   seiner [ess isst zine-uh]
hit: he hit me er hat mich geschlagen [air hat
   mish geh-shlah-ghen]
hitch-hike trampen [trempen]
   hitch-hiker der Anhalter
Hochgarage *multi-storey car park*
Höchstgeschwindigkeit *maximum speed*
hold halten
hole das Loch [lok]
holiday der Urlaub [oor-lōwp]
   (student's) die Ferien [fay-ree-en]
   I'm on holiday ich bin im Urlaub/in Ferien
Holland Holland [holl-annt]
home das Zuhause [tsoo-hōw-zuh]
   I want to go home ich möchte nach Hause [ish
   murrshtuh nahk hōw-zuh]
   at home zu Hause
   I'm homesick ich habe Heimweh [ish
   hah-buh hime-vay]
honest ehrlich [air-lish]
   honestly? ehrlich?
honey der Honig [hoh-nik]
honeymoon die Hochzeitsreise
   [hock-tsites-ry-zuh]
hope die Hoffnung [hoff-noong]
   I hope that . . . ich hoffe, daß . . . [ish hoff-uh
   dass]
   I hope so/not hoffentlich/hoffentlich nicht!
   [hoff-ent-lish]
horizon der Horizont [horee-tsonnt]
horn *(car)* die Hupe [hoo-puh]
horrible schrecklich [–lish]
hors d'oeuvre das Hors d'oeuvre
horse das Pferd [pfairt]

hospital das Krankenhaus [–hōws]
» *TRAVEL TIP: reciprocal health agreement gives free hospital treatment in Germany; forms from your local DHSS*
host der Gastgeber [–gay-ber]
hostess die Gastgeberin *(air)* die Hosteß
hot heiß [hice] *(spiced)* scharf
hotel das Hotel
hotplate die Wärmplatte [vairm-plat-uh]
hot-water bottle die Wärmflasche [–flash-uh]
hour eine Stunde [shtoon-duh]
house das Haus [hōws]
　housewife eine Hausfrau [–frōw]
how wie [vee]
　how many wieviele [vee-feel-uh]
　how much wieviel [vee-feel]
　how often wie oft
　how long wie lange [. . . lang-uh]
　how long have you been here? seit wann sind Sie da? [zite van zinnt zee dah]
　how are you? wie geht's? [vee gayts]
humid feucht [foysht]
humour der Humor [hoo-mor]
hundredweight der Zentner [tsent-ner]
» *TRAVEL TIP: 1 cwt = 50.8 kilos*
hungry hungrig [hoon-grik]
　I'm hungry/not hungry ich habe Hunger/ich habe keinen Hunger [ish hah-buh hoong-er/. . . kine-en . . .]
hupen sound your horn
hurry: I'm in a hurry ich habe es eilig [ish hah-buh ess eye-lik]
　please hurry! bitte beeilen Sie sich! [bittuh buh-eye-len zee zish]
hurt: it hurts es tut weh [ess toot vay]
　my leg hurts mein Bein tut mir weh [mine bine toot meer vay]
　YOU MAY HEAR . . .
　ist es ein stechender Schmerz? [isst ess ine shtek-ender shmairts] *is it a sharp pain?*
husband: my husband mein Mann [mine . . .]

I ich [ish] **I am** ich bin
ice das Eis [ice]
　ice-axe der Eispickel
　ice-cream das Eis
　iced coffee der Eiskaffee [–kaff-ay]
　with lots of ice mit viel Eis [mit feel . . .]
identity papers die Ausweispapiere
　[ōws-vice-pap-ee-ruh]
idiot der Idiot [id-ee-oht]
if wenn [ven]
ignition die Zündung [tsōōn-dŏong]
ill krank; **I feel ill** ich fühle mich nicht wohl
　[ish fōō-luh mish nisht vohl]
illegal illegal [ill-ay-gahl]
illegible unleserlich [ŏon-lay-zair-lish]
illness die Krankheit [–hite]
Imbiß(stube) *snack bar*
immediately sofort [zohfort]
import der Import
important wichtig [vik-tik]
　it's very important es ist sehr wichtig [ess isst
　zair . . .]
import duty der Einfuhrzoll [ine-foor-tsoll]
impossible unmöglich [ŏon-murr-glish]
impressive beeindruckend [buh-ine-drŏok-ent]
improve verbessern [fairbessern]
　I want to improve my German ich möchte
　besser Deutsch lernen [ish murrshtuh besser
　doytsh lair-nen]
in in
inch der Zoll [tsoll]
»　*TRAVEL TIP: 1 inch = 2.54 cm*
include einschließen [ine-shlee-sen]
　does that include breakfast? ist Frühstück
　inbegriffen? [isst frōō-shtŏok in-buh–]
inclusive inklusive [in-kloo-zee-vuh]
incompetent unfähig [ŏon-fay-ik]
inconsiderate unaufmerksam
　[ŏon-owf-mairk-zahm]
incredible unglaublich [ŏon-glowp-lish]
indecent unanständig [ŏon-an-shtendik]

independent unabhängig [ŏon-app-heng-i*k*]
India Indien [in-dee-un]
Indian indisch
   (person) Inder; *(woman)* Inderin
indicator der Blinker
indigestion die Magenverstimmung
   [m*a*h-ghen-fair-shtim-ŏong]
indoors drinnen
industry die Industrie [in-dŏos-tree]
infection die Infektion [in-fekts-ee-*o*hn]
infectious ansteckend [*a*n-shteck-ent]
inflation die Inflation [in-flats-ee-*o*hn]
informal zwanglos [tsvang-lohs]; *(dress)* leger
   [lay-j*air*]; *(agreement)* inform*e*ll
information Informationen
   [in-for-mats-ee-*o*h-nen]
   **do you have any information in English
   about . . .?** haben Sie Informationsmaterial in
   Englisch über . . .? [. . .–mah-tay-ree-ahl in
   eng-glish ŏober]
   is there an information office? gibt es da
   eine Informationsstelle? [gheept ess dah ine-uh
   –shtelluh]
inhabitant der Einwohner [*ine*-voh-nuh]
injection die Spritze [shprits-uh]
injured verletzt [fair-l*e*tst]
   he's been injured er ist verletzt
injury die Verletzung [fair-l*e*ts-ŏong]
innocent unschuldig [ŏon-sh*o*ol-di*k*]
insect ein Ins*e*kt [inz*e*kt]
inside innen
insist: I insist (on it) ich bestehe darauf [ish
   buh-sht*ay*-uh dah-r*o*wf]
insomnia die Schlaflosigkeit [shl*a*f-lohs-i*k*-kite]
instant coffee der Pulverkaffee
   [p*oo*l-ver-kaff-ay]
instead statt dessen [shtatt . . .]
   instead of anstelle von [an-sht*e*l-uh fon]
insulating tape das Isolierband
insulation die Isolierung [eez-oh-leerŏong]
insult die Beleidigung [buh-l*i*de-ee-gŏong]

....

insurance die Versicherung [fair-*zi*sh-er*oo*ng]
intelligent intelligent [–gh*e*nt]
interesting interessant [–*a*nt]
international international
[inter-nats-ee-oh-n*a*hl]
**interpret: would you interpret for
us?** würden Sie für uns dolmetschen? [v*oo*rden
zee f*oo*r *oo*nts d*o*ll-met-shen]
into in
introduce: can I introduce . . .? darf
ich . . . vorstellen? [. . . for-shtellen]
invalid (*noun*) der Kranke [–kuh]
  (*disabled*) der Invalide [in-val-*ee*duh]
  invalid chair der Rollstuhl [rol-shtool]
invitation die Einladung [*ine*-lah-d*oo*ng]
  thank you for the invitation danke für die
  Einladung [dankuh f*oo*r dee . . .]
invite: can I invite you out tonight? kann ich
  Sie für heute abend einladen? [kan ish zee f*oo*r
  hoytuh ah-bent *ine*-la-den]
invoice die Rechnung [r*e*sh-n*oo*ng]
Ireland Irland [*eer*-lannt]
Irish irisch [*eer*-ish]
  (*person*) Ire [*eer*uh]; (*woman*) Irin [*eer*in]
iron (*verb*) bügeln [b*oo*-geln]
  (*noun*) das Bügeleisen [–eye-zen]
  will you iron these for me? würden Sie diese
  für mich bügeln? [v*oo*rden zee deez-uh f*oo*r
  mish . . .]
ironmonger's die (Eisen- und)
  Haushaltswarenhandlung [eye-zen *oo*nt
  h*oo*wss-halts-vah-ren-h*a*nnt-l*oo*ng]
is ist [isst]
island die Insel [*in*-zel]
it es [ess]
Italian italienisch [it-al-ee-*ay*-nish]
  (*person*) Italiener; (*woman*) Italienerin
Italy Italien [i-t*a*hl-ee-un]
itch ein Jucken [y*oo*cken]
  it itches es juckt [. . . y*oo*ckt]
itemize: would you itemize it for me? würden

Sie dies für mich aufschlüsseln? [vōōrden zee
dees fōōr mish ōwf-shlōōs-eln]
jack der Wagenheber [vah-ghen-hay-ber]
jacket die Jacke [yack-uh]
  (of man's suit) das Jackett
jam die Marmelade [mar-meh-lah-duh]
  traffic jam der (Verkehrs)stau
  [fair-kayrs-shtōw]
January Januar [yan-oo-ar]
jaw der Kiefer [kee-fer]
jealous eifersüchtig [eye-fair-zōōk-tik]
jeans die Jeans
jellyfish die Qualle [kvalluh]
jetty der Pier
jewellery der Schmuck [shmoock]
job die Arbeit [ar-bite]
  just the job goldrichtig [gollt-rik-tik]
joke *(noun)* der Witz [vits]
  you must be joking das soll wohl ein Witz
  sein [dass zol vohl ine vits zine]
journey die Reise [ry-zuh]
  have a good journey gute Reise [goot-uh . . .]
July Juli [yoo-lee]
jumper der Pullover
jump leads ein Starthilfekabel
  [–hill-fuh-kah-bel]
junction die Kreuzung [kroy-tsoong]
June Juni [yoo-nee]
junk der Ramsch [ramsh]
just: just two nur zwei [noor tsvy]
  just a little nur ein wenig [. . . vayn-ik]
  just there genau dort [gheh-nōw . . .]
  that's just right das ist gerade richtig [dass
  isst gheh-rah-duh rik-tik]
  not just now jetzt nicht [yets nisht]
  just now jetzt
  he was here just now er war gerade hier [air
  var gheh-rah-duh heer]
kalt *cold*
Kasse *cash desk*
keen begeistert [buh-ghy-stert]

....

I'm not keen ich bin nicht wild darauf [ish bin nisht vilt dar*o*wf]

keep: can I keep it? kann ich es behalten? [. . . buh-halten]

you keep it Sie können es behalten [zee kurr*n*en . . .]

keep the change der Rest ist für Sie [dair rest isst f*oo*r zee]

you didn't keep your promise Sie haben Ihr Versprechen nicht gehalten [zee hah-ben eer fair-shpr*e*shen nisht geh-halten]

it keeps on breaking es geht dauernd kaputt [ess gayt d*o*w-ernt . . .]

kein Durchgang für Fußgänger *no pedestrians*

kein Trinkwasser *not for drinking*

kein Zutritt (für Unbefugte) *no admittance (for unauthorised persons)*

kettle der Kessel

key der Schlüssel [shl*oo*s-el]

kidney die Niere [nee-ruh]

kill töten [turr-ten]

kilo ein Kilo

» *TRAVEL TIP: conversion:* $\frac{kilos}{5} \times 11 = pounds$

kilos	1	1½	5	6	7	8	9
pounds	2.2	3.3	11	13.2	15.4	17.6	19.8

kilometre ein Kilometer [–may-ter]

» *TRAVEL TIP: conversion:* $\frac{kilometres}{8} \times 5 = miles$

kilometres	1	5	10	20	50	100
miles	0.62	3.11	6.2	12.4	31	62

kind: that's very kind of you das ist sehr freundlich von Ihnen [. . . zair froynt-lish fon ee-nen]

kiss der Kuß [k*oo*ss]

kitchen die Küche [k*oo*-shuh]

knee das Knie [kuh-n*ee*]

knickers der Schlüpfer [shl*oo*p-fer]

knife ein Messer

knock klopfen

there's a knocking noise from the engine

....

der Motor klopft
know wissen [vissen]
(be acquainted with) kennen
I don't know ich weiß nicht [ish vice nisht]
I know him ich kenne ihn [. . . ken-uh een]
Krankenhaus hospital
Kreuzung crossroads
kurvenreiche Strecke bends

label das Etikett
laces *(shoe)* Schnürsenkel [shnōōr-zenkel]
lacquer der Lack
ladies die Damentoilette [dah-men-twa-lettuh]
lady eine Dame [dah-muh]
lager ein helles Bier [. . . beer]
   lager and lime *not a German drink, ask for*
   eine Berliner Weiße (mit Limone) [bair-leen-er
   vice-uh (mit lee-moh-nuh)]
lake der See [zay]
lamb *(meat)* das Lamm
lamp die Lampe [lamp-uh]
   lampshade der Lampenschirm [–sheerm]
   lamp-post der Laternenpfahl
   [lah-tairn-en-pfahl]
land *(noun)* das Land [lannt]
lane *(car)* die Spur [spoor]
langsam fahren drive slowly
language die Sprache [shprah-kuh]
large groß [grohss]
laryngitis die Kehlkopfentzündung
   [kayl-kopf-ent-tsōōn-dōong]
last letzter [lets-ter]
   last year/week letztes Jahr/letzte Woche
   last night gestern abend; *(late)* gestern nacht
   [ghestern ah-bent/nahkt]
   at last! endlich! [ent-lish]
late: sorry I'm late entschuldigen Sie, daß ich
   zu spät komme [ent-shool-dig-en zee dass ish
   tsoo shpayt kommuh]
   it's a bit late es ist ein bißchen spät
   [. . . bis-shen . . .]
   please hurry, I'm late bitte beeilen Sie sich,

....

ich bin spät dran [bittuh-buh-eye-len zee zish
ish bin shpayt dran]
at the latest spätestens [shpayt-es-tenz]
later später [shpayter]
I'll come back later ich komme später zurück
see you later! bis später!
laugh *(verb)* lachen [lah-*k*en]
laundrette die Münzwäscherei
[mōōnts-vesh-er-eye]
» *TRAVEL TIP: not very many of these in Germany;
try a 'Sofortreinigung'*
lavatory die Toilette [twa-lettuh]
law das Gesetz [gheh-zets]
Lawinengefahr *danger of avalanches*
lawyer der Rechtsanwalt [reshts-anvalt]
laxative ein Abführmittel [app-fōōr-mittel]
lay-by der Parkplatz
lazy faul [fōwl]
leaf das Blatt
leak eine undichte Stelle [ōōn-dish-tuh shtel-uh]
it leaks es ist nicht dicht
learn: I want to learn ich möchte . . . lernen
[ish murrshtuh . . . lair-nen]
lease *(verb)* mieten [meeten]
(land, business premises) pachten [pa*k*-ten]
least: not in the least nicht im geringsten
[nisht im gheringsten]
at least mindestens [minn-dess-tenz]
leather das Leder [lay-der]
the meat's like leather dieses Fleisch ist zäh
wie Leder [deez-es flysh isst tsay vee lay-der]
leave: we're leaving tomorrow wir fahren
morgen ab [veer fah-ren . . . app]
when does the bus leave? wann fährt der
Bus? [van fairt dair bōōss]
I left two shirts in my room ich habe zwei
Hemden in meinem Zimmer liegenlassen [ish
hah-buh tsvy . . . lee-ghen-lassen]
can I leave this here? kann ich das
hierlassen? [. . . heerlassen]
Lebensgefahr *danger*

....

left linke; **on the left** links
  to be left-handed Linkshänder sein
  [links-hender zine]
left luggage (office) die Gepäckaufbewahrung
  [gheh-peck-ōwf-buh-vah-rōong]
leg das Bein [bine]
legal legal [lay-gahl]
  legal aid die Rechtshilfe [reshts-hil-fuh]
lemon die Zitrone [tsi-troh-nuh]
lemonade eine Limonade [lee-moh-na-duh]
lend: will you lend me your . . .? leihen Sie
  mir Ihr . . .? [lye-en zee meer eer . . .]
lengthen verlängern [fair-lengern]
  (clothes) länger machen [lenger mah-ken]
lens *(of glasses)* das Glas [glahss]
  (camera) das Objektiv [opp-yek-teef]
Lent die Fastenzeit [fass-ten-tsite]
less weniger [vay-nee-gher]
let: let me help darf ich Ihnen helfen?
  [. . . ee-nen . . .]
  let me go! lassen Sie mich los! [. . . lohs]
  will you let me off here würden Sie mich hier
  aussteigen lassen [vōorden zee mish heer
  ōws-shty-ghen . . .]
  let's go gehen wir! [gay-en veer]
letter der Brief [breef]
  are there any letters for me? habe ich Post?
  [hah-buh ish posst]
  letterbox der Briefkasten [breefkasten]
» *TRAVEL TIP: letterboxes are yellow*
lettuce ein Kopfsalat [kopf-za-laht]
level-crossing der Bahnübergang
  [bahn-ōober-gang]
liable *(responsible)* haftbar
library die Bibliothek [bee-blee-oh-tayk]
licence die Genehmigung [gheh-nay-mee-gōong]
lid der Deckel
lie *(noun)* eine Lüge [lōo-guh]
  can he lie down for a bit? kann er sich ein
  bißchen hinlegen? [kan air zish ine bis-shen
  hin-lay-ghen]

....

life das Leben [lay-ben]
  life assurance die Lebensversicherung
  [lay-benz-fair-zish-er-oong]
  not at my time of life! nicht in meinem Alter!
  [nisht in mine-em al-ter]
  lifebelt der Rettungsgürtel [ret-oongs-göörtel]
  lifeboat das Rettungsboot [–boht]
  life-guard der Bademeister
  [bah-duh-my-ster]
  (on beach) der Rettungsschwimmer
  [–shvimmer]
  life-jacket eine Schwimmweste
  [schvim-vest-uh]
lift: do you want a lift? kann ich Sie
  mitnehmen? [kan ish zee mit-nay-men]
  could you give me a lift? könnten Sie mich
  mitnehmen? [kurrnten . . .]
  the lift isn't working der Fahrstuhl ist außer
  Betrieb [. . . fahr-shtool isst öwsser buh-treep]
light das Licht [lisht]
  (not heavy) leicht [lysht]
  the lights aren't working das Licht geht
  nicht [. . . gayt nisht]
  (car) die Scheinwerfer funktionieren nicht
  [shine-vairfer foonk-tsee-ohn-ee-ren . . .]
  have you got a light? haben Sie Feuer?
  [hah-ben zee foy-er]
  when it gets light wenn es hell wird
  [ven . . . virt]
  light bulb die Glühbirne [glöö-beer-nuh]
  light meter der Belichtungsmesser
  [buh-lish-toongs-messer]
like: would you like . . .? möchten Sie . . .?
  [murrshten zee]
  I'd like a . . ./I'd like to . . . ich hätte gerne
  ein . . ./ich würde gerne . . . [ish hett-uh
  gairn-uh ine/vöorduh . . .]
  I like it/you das gefällt mir/ich mag Sie gern
  [dass gheh-felt meer/ish mahg zee gairn]
  I don't like it das gefällt mir nicht [gheh-felt
  meer nisht]

....

like this one wie dieser [vee dee-zer]
what's it like? wie ist es? [vee . . .]
do it like this machen Sie es so [mah-*k*en zee ess zoh]
lime die Limone [lee-*m*oh-nuh]
line die Linie [*lee*-nee-uh]
lip die Lippe [lip-uh]
lipstick der Lippenstift [–shtift]
liqueur ein Likör [lik-urr]
list *(noun)* die Liste [list-uh]
listen zuhören [ts*oo*-hurr-ren]
listen! hören Sie zu! [hurr-ren zee ts*oo*]
litre der Liter [*lee*-ter]
» *TRAVEL TIP: 1 litre = 1¾ pints = 0.22 gals*
little klein [kline]
a little ice/a little more ein wenig Eis/noch ein wenig [ine vay-ni*k* ice/no*k* . . .]
just a little nur ein wenig, nur ein bißchen [noor . . . bis-shen]
live leben [l*ay*-ben]
I live in . . . ich wohne in [ish voh-nuh . . .]
where do you live? wo wohnen Sie? [voh voh-nen zee]
liver die Leber [l*ay*-ber]
LKW = Lastkraftwagen *lorry, truck*
loaf ein Brot [broht]
lobster ein Hummer [h*oo*mmer]
local: could we try a local wine? können wir einen Wein aus der Gegend probieren? [kurrnen veer ine-en vine *ō*wss dair g*ay*-ghent proh-b*ee*-ren]
a local restaurant ein Restaurant im Ort [. . . res-tor-rong . . .]
is it made locally? wird es hier hergestellt? [virt ess heer h*air*-gheh-shtelt]
lock: the lock's broken das Schloß ist kaputt [. . . shloss . . .]
I've locked myself out ich habe mich ausgeschlossen [ish hah-buh mish *ō*wss-gheh-shlossen]
lonely einsam [ine-zahm]

....

long lang
> **we'd like to stay longer** wir würden gerne
> etwas länger bleiben [veer vōōrden gairn-uh
> etvass leng-er bly-ben]
> **that was long ago** das ist lange her [. . .
> lang-uh hair]

loo: where's the loo? wo ist das Klo? [voh . . .
kloh]

look: you look tired Sie sehen müde aus [zee
zay-en mōō-duh ōwss]
> **I'm looking forward to . . .** ich freue mich
> auf . . . [ish froy-uh mish ōwf]
> **I'm looking for . . .** ich suche . . . [ish zook-uh]
> **I'm just looking** ich möchte mich nur
> umschauen [ish murrsh-tuh mish noor
> oom-shōw-en]
> **look at that** schauen Sie sich das an! [shōw-en
> zee zish dass an]
> **look out!** Vorsicht! [for-zisht]

loose lose [loh-zuh]

lorry der Last(kraft)wagen, der Lkw
[lasst(krafft)vah-ghen, el-kah-vay]
> **lorry-driver** der Lkw-Fahrer

lose verlieren [fair-lee-ren]
> **I've lost my . . .** ich habe mein . . . verloren
> [ish hah-buh mine . . . fair-lor-ren]
> **excuse me, I'm lost** entschuldigen Sie, ich
> habe mich verlaufen [ent-shool-dig-en zee ish
> hah-buh mish fair-lōwf-en]
> *(driving)* ich habe mich verfahren
> [. . . fair-fah-ren]
> **lost property office** das Fundbüro
> [foont-bōō-roh]

lot: a lot/not a lot viel/nicht viel [feel]
> **a lot of chips/wine** eine Menge Pommes
> Frites/Wein [ine-uh meng-uh pom freet/vine]
> **lots of** jede Menge [yay-duh . . .]
> **a lot more expensive** viel teurer [feel toy-rer]

lotion die Lotion [lohts-ee-ohn]

loud laut [lōwt]; **louder** lauter [lōwter]

love: I love you ich liebe dich [ish lee-buh dish]

he's in love er ist verliebt [air isst fair-leept]
I love this wine ich mag diesen Wein sehr
gern [ish mahg dee-zen vine zair gairn]
do you love me? liebst du mich? [leepst doo
mish]
lovely schön [shurrn]
low niedrig [nee-drik]
luck das Glück [glŏŏck]
  good luck! viel Glück! [feel glŏŏck]
lucky Glücks- [glŏŏcks-]
  you're lucky Sie haben Glück [zee hah-ben
glŏŏck]
  that's lucky das ist Glück [dass isst . . .]
luggage das Gepäck [gheh-peck]
lumbago der Hexenschuß [hexen-shooss]
lump die Beule [boy-luh]
  (inside) die Geschwulst [gheh-shvoolst]
lunch das Mittagessen [mi-tahg-essen]
lung die Lunge [loong-uh]
Luxembourg Luxemburg [looxemboorg]
luxurious luxuriös [loox-oo-ree-urrs]
luxury der Luxus [loox-ooss]
machine die Maschine [mash-ee-nuh]
mad verrückt [fair-rŏŏckt]
madam gnädige Frau [guh-nay-dig-uh frŏw]
made-to-measure nach Maß [nahk mahss]
magazine die Zeitschrift [tsite-shrift]
magnificent großartig [grohss-ahr-tik]
maiden name der Mädchenname
[maid-shen-nah-muh]
mail die Post [posst]; **is there any mail for
me?** habe ich Post? [hah-buh ish . . .]
main road die Hauptstraße
[hŏwpt-shtrahss-uh]
make machen [mah-ken]
  will we make it in time? schaffen wir das
rechtzeitig? [shaffen veer dass resht-tsytik]
  make-up das Make-up
man der Mann
manager der Geschäftsführer
[gheh-shefts-fŏŏr-er]

....

can I see the manager? kann ich mit dem Geschäftsführer sprechen? [. . . shpreshen]

manicure die Maniküre [man-ee-k$\overline{oo}$-ruh]

manners die Manieren [man-*ee*-ren]

many viele [feel-uh]

map die Karte [kar-tuh]; **a map of . . .** eine Karte von . . . [ine-uh kar-tuh fon]

March März [mairts]

margarine die Margarine [mar-ga-re*en*-uh]

marina der Jachthafen [ya*k*t-hah-fen]

mark: there's a mark on it es ist beschädigt [. . . buh-sh*a*y-di*k*t]

(stained) da ist ein Fleck darauf [dah-r$\overline{o}$wf]

market der Markt

  marketplace der Marktplatz

marmalade die Orangenmarmelade [or*o*n-djen-mar-meh-lah-duh]

married verheiratet [fair-hy-raht-et]

marry: will you marry me? willst du mich heiraten? [villst doo mish hy-rahten]

marvellous wunderbar [v*oo*nderbar]

mascara die Wimperntusche [vimpern-t*oo*sh-uh]

mashed potatoes der Kartoffelbrei [kartoffel-bry]

massage eine Massage [massah-djuh]

mast der Mast [masst]

mat die Matte [mat-uh]

match: a box of matches eine Schachtel Streichhölzer [sha*k*-tel shtrysh-hurltser]

  football match ein Fußballspiel [fooss-bal-shpeel]

material das Material [ma-tay-ree-*a*hl]

matter: it doesn't matter das macht nichts [dass mah*k*t nix]

  what's the matter? was ist los? [vass isst lohs]

mattress die Matratze [ma-tr*a*ts-uh]

mature reif [rife]

maximum maximal [maxi-mahl]

(noun) das Maximum [maxim*oo*m]

  that's our maximum offer das ist unser

höchstes Angebot [. . . ŏonz-er hurrk-stess
an-gheh-boht]

May Mai [my]

may: may I have . . . ? darf ich . . . haben
[. . . ish . . . hah-ben]

maybe vielleicht [fee lysht]

mayonnaise die Mayonnaise [my-on-ay-zuh]

me mich [mish]

    with/from me mit/von mir [. . . fon meer]

    give it to me geben Sie es mir

    it was me ich war es [ish var ess]

meal das Essen

mean: what does this mean? was heißt das?
[vass hysst dass]

    by all means! aber natürlich [ah-ber
natōr-lish]

measles die Masern [mah-zern]

    German measles die Röteln [rurr-teln]

measurements die Maße [mahss-uh]

meat das Fleisch [flysh]

mechanic: is there a mechanic here? gibt es
hier einen Mechaniker? [gheept ess heer ine-en
meck-ahn-iker]

medicine die Medizin [medi-tseen]

meet treffen

    pleased to meet you angenehm!
[an-gheh-naym]

meeting die Besprechung [buh-shpresh-ŏong]
    (conference) die Sitzung [zitsŏong]

melon eine Melone [meh-loh-nuh]

member das Mitglied [mit-gleet]

    how do I become a member? wie werde ich
Mitglied? [vee vair-duh ish mit-gleet]

men die Männer [men-er]

mend: can you mend this? können Sie dies
flicken? [kurrnen zee dees . . .]

mention: don't mention it gern geschehen
[gairn gheh-shay-en]

menu die Speisekarte [shpy-zuh-kar-tuh]

    can I have the menu, please? kann ich, bitte,
die Speisekarte haben?

....

Vorspeisen Hors d'oeuvre
Geräucherter Aal *smoked eel*
Königspastete *chicken vol-au-vent*
Krabbencocktail: *prawn cocktail*
Meefischli *small fried fish from River Main*
Weinbergschnecken *snails*

Suppen Soups
Blumenkohlsuppe *cream of cauliflower*
Brotsuppe *(Black Forest) bread soup*
Flädlesuppe *(Swabia) consommé with pancake strips*
Hühnerbrühe *chicken broth*
Klößchensuppe *clear soup with dumplings*
Kraftbrühe mit Ei *consommé with a raw egg*
Ochsenschwanzsuppe *oxtail soup*
Tagessuppe *soup of the day*

Vom Rind Beef
Bouletten *(Berlin) meat balls*
Deutsches Beefsteak *mince patty*
Rinderbraten *pot roast*
Rinderfilet *fillet steak*
Rindsrouladen *beef olives*
Rostbraten *(Swabia) steak with onions*
Sauerbraten *marinaded potroast beef*

Vom Schwein Pork
Eisbein *knuckles of pork*
Karbonade *(Berlin) roast ribs of pork*
Kotelett *chops*
Leberkäse *(South Ger) baked pork and beef loaf*
Schweinebraten *roast pork*
Schweineschnitzel *pork fillets*

Vom Kalb Veal
Gefüllte Kalbsbrust *veal roll*
Kalbshaxe *leg of veal*
Jägerschnitzel *veal with mushrooms*
Wienerschnitzel *veal in breadcrumbs*
Zigeunerschnitzel *veal with peppers and relishes*

Wild Game
Rehbraten *roast venison*
Wildschweinsteak *wild boar steak*

Fischgerichte Fish
Forelle Müllerin *trout with butter and lemon*
Hecht *pike*
Karpfen blau *boiled blue carp*
Matjesheringe *pickled herrings*

Bockwurst *large Frankfurter sausage*
Bratwurst *grilled pork sausage*
Halbes Hähnchen *half a (roast) chicken*

Spezialitäten Specialities
Himmel und Erde *(Rhineland) potatoes and
apple sauce with black pudding*
Kohl und Pinkel *(Bremen) cabbage and potatoes
with sausages and smoked meat*
Labskaus *(Hamburg) potatoes mixed with pieces
of fish and meat*
Weißwürste mit Senf *(Munich) white sausages
and sweet mustard*

Beilagen Side dishes
Blumenkohl *cauliflower;* Bratkartoffeln *roast
potatoes;* Erbsen *peas;* gemischter Salat
mixed salad; Gemüseplatte *mixed veg;*
Kartoffelpüree *mashed potatoes;* Klöße,
Knödel *dumplings;* Pommes Frites
French fried potatoes; Rosenkohl
Brussel sprouts; Salzkartoffel *boiled potatoes;*
Sauerkraut *finely chopped
pickled cabbage;* Spargel *asparagus;*
Spätzle *homemade noodles*

Nachspeisen Desserts
Gemischtes Eis mit Sahne *assorted ice creams
with whipped cream*
Eisbecher *knickerbocker glory*
Obstsalat *fruit salad*
Rote Grütze *(North Germany) fruit blancmange*

mess ein Durcheinander [doorsh-ine-ander]

message: are there any messages for me?
hat jemand eine Nachricht für mich
hinterlassen? [. . . yay-mannt ine-uh
nah*k*-risht foor mish . . .]

can I leave a message for . . .? kann ich eine
Nachricht für . . . hinterlassen?

metre der Meter [may-ter]

» *TRAVEL TIP: 1 metre = 39.37 ins = 1.09 yds*

midday der Mittag [mi-tahg]

middle die Mitte [mittuh]

in the middle in der Mitte [in dair mittuh]

midnight Mitternacht [mitter-nah*k*t]

might: I might be wrong vielleicht hab' ich
unrecht [fee-lysht hahb ish oon-resht]

he might have gone er ist vielleicht schon
gegangen [air isst fee-lysht shohn
gheh-gang-en]

migraine die Migräne [mee-grain-uh]

mild mild [milt]

mile die Meile [my-luh]

» *TRAVEL TIP: conversion:* $\dfrac{miles}{5} \times 8 = kilometres$

miles	½	1	3	5	10	50	100
kilometres	0.8	1.6	4.8	8	16	80	160

milk die Milch [milsh]

a glass of milk ein Glas Milch

milkshake das Milchmixgetränk
[milsh-mix-gheh-trenk]

millimetre der Millimeter [–mayter]

milometer der Kilometerzähler
[kilo-mayter-tsayler]

minced meat das Hackfleisch [hack-flysh]

mind: I've changed my mind ich habe es mir
anders überlegt [ish ha*h*-buh ess meer anders
ooberlaygt]

I don't mind das macht mir nichts aus [dass
mah*k*t meer nix meers]

do you mind if I . . .? macht es Ihnen etwas
aus, wenn ich . . .? [mah*k*t ess ee-nen et-vass
owss ven ish . . .]

never mind macht nichts [mah*k*t nix]
mine mein [mine]
mineral water das Mineralwasser
[minerahl-vasser]
minimum das Minimum [minim*oo*m]
minus minus [m*ee*-n*oo*ss]
minute die Minute [min*oo*-tuh]
   he'll be here in a minute er kommt gleich
   [air ... glysh]
   just a minute einen Moment, bitte [ine-en
   moh-ment bittuh]
mirror der Spiegel [shp*ee*-ghel]
Miss Fräulein [froy-line]
miss: I miss you du fehlst mir [doo faylst meer]
   he's missing er ist verschwunden [air isst
   fair-shv*oo*nden]
   there's a ... missing da fehlt ein ... [dah
   faylt ine ...]
mist der Nebel [naybel]
mistake ein Fehler [fayler]
   I think you've made a mistake ich glaube,
   Sie haben sich vertan [ish gl*ow*-buh zee
   h*a*h-ben zish fair-t*a*n]
misunderstanding ein Mißverständnis
[m*i*ss-fair-shtent-niss]
modern modern [mod*ai*rn]
Monday Montag [mohntahg]
money das Geld [gelt]
   I've lost my money ich habe mein Geld
   verloren [ish hah-buh mine gelt fair-l*o*r-ren]
   no money kein Geld [kine gelt]
month der Monat [moh-naht]
moon der Mond [mohnt]
moped das Moped
more mehr [mair]
   can I have some more? kann ich noch etwas
   haben? [kan ish n*o*k et-vass h*a*h-ben]
   more wine, please noch ein wenig Wein, bitte
   [n*o*k ine vayni*k* vine bittuh]
   no more nicht mehr [nisht mair]
   more comfortable bequemer [buh-kv*a*y-mer]

....

more than mehr als [mair alz]

morning der Morgen [mor-ghen]

  this morning heute morgen [hoy-tuh . . .]

  good morning guten Morgen [gooten . . .]

  in the morning morgens [morghenz]

most: I like it/you most das gefällt/Sie gefallen
mir am besten [. . . gheh-fellt/zee gheh-fal-en
meer . . .]

  most of the time/most of the people
meistens/die meisten Leute [my-stenz/dee
my-sten loy-tuh]

mother: my mother meine Mutter [mine-uh
mooter]

motor der Motor

motorbike das Motorrad [–raht]

motorboat das Motorboot [–boht]

motorcyclist der Motorradfahrer
[motor-raht-fah-rer]

motorist der Autofahrer [ōw-toh-fah-rer]

motorway die Autobahn [ōw-toh-bahn]

mountain der Berg [bairk]

  mountaineer ein Bergsteiger [–shtyger]

  mountaineering das Bergsteigen [–shtygen]

mouse die Maus [mōwss]

moustache der Schnurrbart [shnoor-bahrt]

mouth der Mund [moont]

move: don't move bewegen Sie sich nicht!
[buh-vay-ghen zee zish nisht]

  could you move your car? könnten Sie Ihren
Wagen wegfahren? [kurrnten zee ee-ren
vah-ghen vek-fahren]

Mr Herr [hair]

Mrs Frau [frōw]

Ms Frau [frōw]

much viel [feel]

  much better/much more viel besser/viel
mehr [feel . . ./feel mair]

  not much nicht viel [nisht feel]

mug: I've been mugged ich bin überfallen
worden [ish bin ōober-fal-en vorden]

mum: my mum meine Mutti [moo-tee]

....

muscle der Muskel [mooss-kel]
museum das Museum [moo-zay-oom]
mushroom der Pilz [pillts]
music die Musik [moozeek]
must: I must ich muß [ish mooss]
  I must not eat . . . ich darf . . . nicht essen [ish
  darf . . . nisht . . .]
  you must do it Sie müssen es tun [zee müssen
  ess toon]
mustard der Senf [zenf]
MWSt = Mehrwertsteuer VAT
my mein [mine]
nail *(finger, wood)* der Nagel [nah-ghel]
  nailfile die Nagelfeile [–fy-luh]
  nail polish der Nagellack [–lack]
  nail clippers der Nagelzwicker [–tsvicker]
  nail scissors die Nagelschere [–shay-ruh]
naked nackt
name der Name [nah-muh]
  my name is . . . ich heiße . . . [ish hyss-uh . . .]
  what's your name? wie heißen Sie? [vee
  hyssen zee]
napkin die Serviette [zair-vee-ettuh]
nappy die Windel [vindel]
  nappy liners die Windeleinlagen
  [vindel-ine-lah-ghen]
narrow eng
national national [nats-ee-oh-nahl]
nationality die Nationalität
  [nats-ee-oh-nahl-ee-tayt]
natural natürlich [natœrlish]
naughty: don't be naughty sei nicht frech [zy
  nisht fresh]
near: is it near? ist es in der Nähe? [isst ess in
  dair nay-uh]
  near here hier herum [heer hairoom]
  do you go near . . .? kommen Sie in die Nähe
  von . . .? [. . . zee in dee nay-uh fon]
  where's the nearest . . .? wo ist der (die/das)
  nächste . . .? [voh ist dair (dee/dass) nex-tuh]
nearly fast [fasst]

....

neat *(drink)* pur [poor]
necessary notwendig [noht-vendi*k*]
 it's not necessary das ist nicht notwendig
neck der Hals [halz]
 necklace das Halsband [halz-bannt]
need: I need a . . . ich brauche einen . . . [ish
 brow*k*-uh ine-en . . .]
needle die Nadel [n*a*h-del]
negotiations die Verhandlungen
 [fair-hannt-l∞ng-en]
neighbour der Nachbar [nah*k*-bar]
neither: neither of them keiner von beiden
 [kine-er fon by-den]
 neither . . . nor . . . weder . . . noch . . .
 [vayder . . . no*k* . . .]
 neither do I ich auch nicht [ish ōw*k* nisht]
nephew: my nephew mein Neffe [mine neffuh]
nervous nervös [nair-vurrs]
net das Netz
 net price der Nettopreis [–price]
never niemals [n*ee*-malz]
 well I never! nein, so was! [nine zoh vass]
new neu [noy]
news die Nachrichten [nah*k*-rishten]
 newsagent der Zeitungshändler
 [tsyt∞ngs-henntler]
 newspaper die Zeitung [tsyt∞ng]
 do you have any English newspapers?
 haben Sie englische Zeitungen? [hah-ben zee
 eng-glish-uh tsyt∞ng-en]
New Year Neujahr [noy-yahr]
 New year's Eve Silvester
 Happy New Year! ein gutes neues Jahr! [ine
 gootes noy-es yahr]
 » *TRAVEL TIP: New Year is celebrated with*
 fireworks and traditionally champagne at
 midnight when people say 'Prosit Neujahr'
 [prohst noy-yahr]; *the next day and afterwards*
 they say 'ein gutes neues Jahr'
New Zealand Neuseeland [noy-zay-lannt]
 New Zealander Neuseeländer [–lender]

(woman) Neuseeländerin

next nächster [nexter]

 please stop at the next corner halten Sie, bitte, an der nächsten Ecke [. . . zee bittuh an dair nexten eckuh]

 see you next year bis nächstes Jahr [bis nextes yahr]

 sit next to me setzen Sie sich neben mich [zet-sen zee zish nay-ben mish]

nice schön [shurrn] *(person)* nett

nicht berühren do not touch

nicht öffnen do not open

Nichtraucher no smoking

niece: my niece meine Nichte [mine-uh nishtuh]

night die Nacht [nah*k*t]

 good night gute Nacht [gootuh nah*k*t]

 at night nachts [nah*k*ts]

 where's a good night club? wo ist ein guter Nachtklub [voh isst ine gooter nah*k*t-klōōb]

 night-life das Nachtleben [nah*k*t-lay-ben]

 night porter der Nachtportier [nah*k*t-por-tee-ay]

no nein [nine]

 there's no water wir haben kein Wasser [veer h*a*h-ben kine vasser]

 no way! auf keinen Fall! [ōwf kine-en fal]

nobody niemand [nee-mannt]

 nobody saw it keiner hat es gesehen [kine-er hat ess gheh-z*a*y-en]

noisy laut [lōwt]

 our room's too noisy in unserem Zimmer ist es zu laut [in œnzerem tsimmer isst ess tsoo . . .]

none keiner [kine-er]; **none of them** keiner von ihnen [kine-er fon ee-nen]

nonsense Quatsch [kvatsh]

normal normal [norm*a*hl]

north der Norden

Northern Ireland Nordirland [nort-*ee*r-lannt]

nose die Nase [nah-zuh]

nosebleed das Nasenbluten [nah-zen-bloo-ten]

....

not nicht [nisht]
  I'm not hungry ich habe keinen Hunger [ish
  hah-buh kine-en hoong-er]
  not that one das nicht [dass nisht]
  not me ich nicht
  I don't understand ich verstehe das nicht [ish
  fair-shtay-uh dass nisht]
  he didn't tell me er hat mir das nicht gesagt
  [air hat meer dass nisht geh-zahgt]
Notausgang *emergency exit*
Notbremse *emergency brake; communication
  cord*
note *(bank note)* der Schein [shine]
nothing nichts [nix]
November November
now jetzt [yetst]
nowhere nirgends [neer-ghenz]
nudist der FKK-Anhänger
  [eff-ka-ka-an-heng-er]
  nudist beach der FKK-Strand [–shtrannt]
nuisance: it's a nuisance das ist ärgerlich
  [dass isst air-guh-lish]
  this man's being a nuisance der Mann
  belästigt mich [. . . buh-lest-ikt mish]
numb taub [tōwp]
number die Zahl [tsahl]
  number plate das Nummernschild
  [noomern-shillt]
nurse die Krankenschwester
  [kranken-shvester]
  (male) der Pfleger [pflay-gher]
nursery slope der Idiotenhügel
  [id-ee-oh-ten-hōō-ghel]
nut die Nuß [nooss]
  (for bolt) die (Schrauben)mutter
  [shrōwben-mooter]
oar das Ruder [rooder]
obligatory obligatorisch [oh-bleegator-ish]
obviously offensichtlich [off-en-zisht-lish]
occasionally gelegentlich [gheh-lay-ghent-lish]
occupied besetzt [buh-zetst]

is this seat occupied? sitzt hier jemand? [zitst heer yay-mannt]

o'clock *see* **time**

October Oktober

odd *(number)* ungerade [oon-gheh-rah-duh]
(strange) seltsam [zelt-zahm]

of von [fon]

off: the milk/meat is off die Milch ist sauer/das Fleisch ist schlecht [dee milsh isst zōw-er/dass flysh isst shlesht]

it just came off es ist einfach abgegangen [. . . ine-fahk app-gheh-gang-en]

10% off 10% Ermäßigung [tsayn proh-tsent air-mace-ee-goong]

office das Büro [bōoroh]

official *(noun)* der Beamte [buh-am-tuh]

Öffnungszeiten opening hours

often oft

oil das Öl [urrl]

I'm losing oil mein Wagen verliert Öl [mine vah-ghen fair-leert urrl]

will you change the oil? könnten Sie, bitte, das Öl wechseln? [kurrnten zee bittuh dass urrl vek-seln]

ointment die Salbe [zahl-buh]

OK okay

old alt; **how old are you?** wie alt sind Sie? [vee alt zinnt zee]

olive die Olive [oh-lee-vuh]

omelette ein Omelett(e) [omuh-lett(uh)]

on auf [ōwf]

I haven't got it on me ich habe es nicht bei mir [ish hah-buh ess nisht by meer]

on Friday am Freitag [am fry-tahg]

on television im Fernsehen [im fairn-zay-en]

once einmal [ine-mahl]

at once sofort [zoh-fort]

one ein [ine] *(number)* eins [ine-ts]

the red one der (die/das) rote [dair (dee/dass) roh-tuh]

onion die Zwiebel [tsvee-bel]

only nur [noor]
  he is the only one er ist der einzige [air isst dair ine-tsig-uh]
open *(adjective)* offen
  (shop) geöffnet [geh-urrf-net]
  I can't open it ich bekomme es nicht auf [ish buh-kommuh ess nisht ōwf]
  when do you open? wann machen Sie auf? [van mah*k*en zee ōwf]
opera die Oper [oh-per]
operation die Operation [oh-per-ats-ee-ohn]
  will I need an operation? muß ich operiert werden? [mœss ish oh-per-eert vairden]
operator *(tel)* die Vermittlung [fair-m*i*tt-lœng]
opposite: opposite the hotel gegenüber dem Hotel [gay-ghen-ōōber daym . . .]
optician der Optiker
or oder [oh-der]
orange die Orange [oronj-uh]
  orange juice der Orangensaft [oronjen-zafft]
order: could we order now? könnten wir jetzt bestellen? [kurrnten veer yetst buh-shtellen]
  thank you, we've already ordered danke, wir haben schon bestellt [dankuh veer h*a*h-ben shohn buh-sht*e*llt]
other: the other one der (die, das) andere [dair (dee, dass) an-der-uh]
  do you have any others? haben Sie irgendwelche anderen? [h*a*h-ben zee irgent-velsh-uh an-der-en]
otherwise sonst
ought: I ought to go ich sollte gehen [ish zolltuh gay-en]
ounce die Unze [œnts-uh]
» *TRAVEL TIP: 1 ounce = 28.35 grammes*
our unser [œn-zer]
  that's ours das ist unseres [. . . œn-zer-es]
out: we're out of petrol uns ist das Benzin ausgegangen [œnz isst dass ben-tseen ōwss-gheh-gang-en]
  get out! raus! [rōwss]

....

outdoors im Freien [im fry-en]

outside: can we sit outside? können wir draußen sitzen? [kurrnen veer drōwssen zitsen]

over: over here/there hier/dort drüben [heer/dort drōben]

  over 40 über vierzig [ōber feer-tsik]

  it's all over es ist aus [ess isst ōwss]

overboard: man overboard! Mann über Bord! [man ōber bort]

overcharge: you've overcharged me Sie haben mir zu viel berechnet [zee hah-ben meer tsoo feel buh-resh-net]

overcooked zu lange gekocht [tsoo lang-uh gheh-kokt]

overexposed überbelichtet [ōber-buh-likt-et]

overnight *(stay, travel)* über Nacht [ōber nahkt]

oversleep verschlafen [fair-shlah-fen]

  I overslept ich habe verschlafen [ish hah-buh fair-shlah-fen]

overtake überholen [ōber-hole-en]

owe: what do I owe you? was bin ich Ihnen schuldig? [vass bin ish ee-nen shooldik]

own *(adjective)* eigen [eye-ghen]

  my own car mein eigenes Auto

  I'm on my own ich bin allein hier [ish bin al-ine heer]

owner der Eigentümer [eye-ghen-tōomer]

oxygen der Sauerstoff [zōw-er-shtoff]

oyster die Auster [ōw-ster]

pack: I haven't packed yet ich habe noch nicht gepackt [ish hah-buh nok nisht gheh-packt]

  can I have a packed lunch? könnte ich ein Lunchpaket haben? [kurrn-tuh ish ine lunch-pa-kayt hah-ben]

package tour die Pauschalreise [pōw-shahl-ry-zuh]

page *(of book)* die Seite [zy-tuh]

  could you page him? können Sie ihn ausrufen lassen? [kurrnen zee een ōwss-roofen . . .]

....

pain der Schmerz [shmairts]
  I've got a pain in my . . . mir tut mein . . . weh
  [meer toot mine . . . vay]
  pain-killers schmerzstillende Mittel
  [shmairts-shtill-end-uh . . .]
painting das Gemälde [gheh-mehl-duh]
pair das Paar [par]
Pakistan Pakistan
Pakistani pakistanisch [–ish]
  (person) Pakistani
pale blaß [blass]
pancake der Pfannkuchen [pfan-kooken]
panties das Höschen [hurrs-shen]
pants die Hose [hoh-zuh]
  (underpants) die Unterhose [oonter-hoh-zuh]
paper das Papier [pa-peer]
  (newspaper) die Zeitung [tsytoong]
parcel das Paket [pa-kayt]
pardon *(didn't understand)* wie bitte? [vee
  bittuh]
  I beg your pardon *(sorry)* Entschuldigung
  [ent-shoold-ee-goong]
parents: my parents meine Eltern
park der Park
  where can I park? wo kann ich parken?
  [voh . . .]
Parken nur mit Parkscheibe *parking discs
required*
Parken verboten *no parking*
Parkplatz *car park*
part ein Teil [ine tile]
partner der Partner
party *(group)* die Gruppe [groop-uh]
  (travel) die Gesellschaft [gheh-zell-shafft]
  (celebration) die Party
  I'm with the . . . party ich bin mit
  der . . . Gruppe hier
pass *(mountain)* der Paß [pas]
passable *(road)* passierbar [pas-eer-bar]
passenger ein Reisender [ry-zender]
  (on ship, plane) ein Passagier [pass-ajeer]

passer-by ein Passant
passport der Paß [pas]
past: in the past früher [frōō-er]
pastry *(dough)* der Teig [tyg]
path der Weg [vayg]
patient: be patient Geduld! [geh-doolt]
pattern das Muster [mooster]
pavement der Gehsteig [gay-shtyg]
pay bezahlen [buh-tsahlen]
   can I pay, please? ich möchte gerne zahlen
   [ish murrshtuh gairn-uh tsahlen]
» *TRAVEL TIP: in bars, pubs etc it's usual to pay*
   when you're leaving and not when you order
pea eine Erbse [erp-suh]
peace der Frieden [free-den]
peach ein Pfirsich [pfeer-zish]
peanuts Erdnüsse [airt-nōōss-uh]
pear eine Birne [beer-nuh]
pebble ein Kieselstein [kee-zel-shtine]
pedal das Pedal [pay-dahl]
pedestrian ein Fußgänger [fooss-genger]
   pedestrian crossing der Fußgängerüberweg
   [fooss-genger-ōōber-vayg]
» *TRAVEL TIP: be warned, the Germans take the red*
   lights for pedestrians rather more seriously than
   we do; on the spot fines can happen
peg der Stift [shtift]
   (for tent) der Hering [hay-ring]
   (mountaineering) der Haken [hah-ken]
pelvis das Becken
pen der Kugelschreiber [kooghel-shryber]
   have you got a pen? haben Sie etwas zum
   Schreiben? [hah-ben zee etvass tsoom shryben]
pencil ein Bleistift [bly-shtift]
penfriend ein Brieffreund [breef-froynt]
penicillin das Penizillin [pen-its-illeen]
penknife das Taschenmesser
pensioner der Rentner
people die Leute [loy-tuh]
   the German people die Deutschen [doyt-shen]

....

pepper der Pfeffer
  green/red pepper der grüne/rote Paprika
  [grōōnuh/roh-tuh . . .]
peppermint das Pfefferminz
per: per night/week/person pro Nacht/
  Woche/Person [proh nah*k*t/vo*k*-uh/pair-zohn]
per cent Prozent [proh-tsent]
perfect perfekt [pair-*f*ekt]
  the perfect holiday der ideale Urlaub [dair
  ee-day-ahl-uh oorlōwp]
perfume das Parfüm [par*f*ōōm]
perhaps vielleicht [fee-lysht]
period der Zeitraum [tsyt-rōwm]
  (medical) die Periode [pay-ree-oh-duh]
perm die Dauerwelle [dōw-er-vell-uh]
permanent dauernd [dōw-ernt]
permit *(noun)* die Genehmigung
  [gheh-n*a*y-migoong] *see* **entry**
person die Person [pair-zohn]
  in person persönlich [pair-zu*rr*n-lish]
petrol das Benzin [ben-ts*ee*n]
  petrol station die Tankstelle [tank-shtell-uh]
» *TRAVEL TIP: 'Super' is 4-star, 'Normal' or 'Benzin'*
  correspond to both 3-star and 2-star
phone *see* **telephone**
photograph die Fotografie [foto-gra-*f*ee]
  would you take a photograph of us?
  würden Sie ein Bild von uns machen? [vōōrden
  zee ine bilt fon oonz mah-*k*en]
piano das Klavier [kla-v*ee*r]
pickpocket der Taschendieb [tashen-deep]
picture ein Bild [bilt]
pie die Pastete [pas-t*a*y-tuh]
  (sweet) der Obstkuchen [ohpst-koo*k*en]
  apple pie der Apfelkuchen [apfel-koo*k*en]
piece das Stück [sht@@ck]; **a piece of cheese**
  ein Stück Käse [ine sht@@ck kay-zuh]
pig das Schwein [shvine]
pigeon die Taube [tōw-buh]
pile-up die Massenkarambolage
  [massen-karambo-l*a*h-juh]

pill eine Tablette [tab-lettuh]
  do you take the pill? nimmst du die Pille?
  [. . . pill-uh]
pillion: on the pillion auf dem Soziussitz [ōwf
  daym zoh-tsee-ooss-zits]
  pillion passenger der Beifahrer [by-fahrer]
pillow das Kissen
pin die (Steck)nadel [(shteck)nah-del]
pineapple eine Ananas
pink *(adjective)* rosa
pint die Pint
» *TRAVEL TIP: 1 pint = 0.57 litres*
pipe die Pfeife [pfy-fuh]
  pipe tobacco der Pfeifentabak
  [pfy-fen-tabak]; *(sink etc)* das Rohr [ror]
piston der Kolben
pity: it's a pity das ist schade [dass isst
  shah-duh]
Pkw [pay-ka-vay] = ***Personenkraftwagen***
  (private) motor car
place der Platz *(town)* der Ort
  is this place taken? ist hier besetzt? [isst heer
  buh-zetst]
  do you know any good places to go? wissen
  Sie, wo man hingehen könnte? [vissen zee voh
  man hin-gay-en kurrnt-uh]
plain *(food)* (gut)bürgerlich
  [(goot)bōōr-gher-gher-lish]
  (not patterned) einfarbig [ine-farbik]
plane das Flugzeug [floog-tsoyg]
plant die Pflanze [pflannts-uh]
  (factory) das Werk [vairk]
  (equipment) die Anlagen [an-lah-ghen]
plaster *(med)* der Gips [ghips] *see* **sticking**
plastic Plastik
plate der Teller
platform der Bahnsteig [bahn-shtyg]
  which platform please? welches Gleis, bitte?
  [velshes glice bittuh]
play *(verb)* spielen [shpeelen]
pleasant angenehm

....

please: could you please . . .? könnten Sie,
bitte, . . .? [kurrnten zee bittuh]
  (yes) please ja, bitte [yah bittuh]
pleasure das Vergnügen [fair-guh-n$\overline{oo}$-ghen]
  my pleasure gern geschehen [gairn gheh-
shay-en]
plenty: plenty of . . . viel . . . [feel]
  thank you, that's plenty danke, das reicht
[dan-kuh dass rysht]
pliers eine Zange [tsang-uh]
plug *(elec)* der Stecker [shtecker]
  (car) die Zündkerze [ts$\overline{oo}$nt-kairts-uh]
  (bathroom) der Stöpsel [shturrp-sel]
plum eine Pflaume [pfl$\overline{ow}$m-uh]
plus plus [pl$\overline{oo}$ss]
p.m. nachmittags [nah*k*-mittahgs]
pneumonia die Lungenentzündung
[l$\overline{oo}$ng-en-ent-ts$\overline{oo}$nd$\overline{oo}$ng]
poached egg ein pochiertes Ei [posheertes eye]
pocket die Tasche [tash-uh]
point: could you point to it? könnten Sie
darauf deuten? [kurrnen zee dar$\overline{ow}$f doyten]
  four point six vier komma sechs [feer . . . zex]
points *(car)* die Unterbrecherkontakte
[$\overline{oo}$nter-br*e*sher-kontakt-uh]
police die Polizei [polits-*e*ye]
  get the police holen Sie die Polizei [hoh-len
zee dee . . .]
  policeman der Polizist [polits-ist]
  police station die (Polizei)wache
[. . . vah*k*-uh]
» *TRAVEL TIP: dial 211*
polish *(noun: shoes)* die Schuhcreme
[sh$\overline{oo}$-kray-muh]
  could you polish my shoes könnten Sie
meine Schuhe putzen lassen? [kurrnten zee
mine-uh sh$\overline{oo}$-uh p$\overline{oo}$tsen lassen]
polite höflich [hurrf-lish]
politics die Politik [poli-t*ee*k]
polluted verschmutzt [fair-shm$\overline{oo}$tst]
polythene bag die Plastiktüte [–t$\overline{oo}$t-uh]

pool *(swimming)* das Schwimmbad [shvimm-baht]

poor: I'm very poor ich bin sehr arm [ish bin zair . . .]; **poor quality** schlechte Qualität [shlekt-uh kval-ee-tayt]

popular beliebt [buh-leept]

population die Bevölkerung [buh-furlk-kuh-roong]

pork das Schweinefleisch [shvine-uh-flysh]

port *(harbour)* der Hafen [hah-fen]
(not starboard) Backbord [–bort]
(drink) der Portwein

porter der Portier [por-tee-ay]
(rail, airport) der Gepäckträger [gheh-peck-tray-gher]

portrait das Porträt [por-tray]

posh vornehm [for-naym]

possible möglich [murr-glish]
could you possibly . . .? könnten Sie eventuell . . .? [kurrn-ten zee ay-vent-oo-el]

post die Post [posst]
postcard die Postkarte [posst-kar-tuh]
post office das Postamt

» *TRAVEL TIP: post offices generally open from 8.00–18.00 Monday to Friday and 8.00 to 12.00 on Saturdays*

poste restante postlagernd [posst-lah-ghernt]

potato die Kartoffel

pottery die Töpferei [turrpfer-eye]
(pots) die Töpferwaren [turrpfer-vah-ren]
(glazed) die Keramik [kay-rah-mik]

pound das Pfund [pfoont]

» *TRAVEL TIP: conversion:* $\frac{pounds}{11} \times 5 = kilos$

pounds	1	3	5	6	7	8	9
kilos	0.45	1.4	2.3	2.7	3.2	3.6	4.1

NB: *a German Pfund = 500 grammes*

pour: it's pouring es gießt [ess geesst]

powder das Pulver [pool-ver]
(face) der Puder [poo-der]

power cut der Stromausfall [shtrohm-ōwss-fal]

power point die Steckdose [shteck-doh-zuh]
prawn cocktail ein Krabbencocktail
prefer: I prefer this one das gefällt mir besser
[. . . gheh-fellt meer . . .]
   I'd prefer to . . . ich würde lieber . . . [ish
vōōr-duh lee-ber]
   I'd prefer a . . . ich hätte lieber ein . . . [ish
het-uh lee-ber ine . . .]
pregnant schwanger [shvanger]
prescription das Rezept [rets-ept]
present: at present zur Zeit [tsoor tsite]
   present company excepted Anwesende
ausgeschlossen [anvay-zend-uh
ōwss-gheh-shlossen]
   here's a present for you ein Geschenk für Sie
[ine gheh-shenk fōōr zee]
president der Präsident [pray-zident]
press: could you press these? könnten Sie sie
bügeln? [kurrnten zee zee bōō-gheln]
pretty hübsch [hōōpsh]
   it's pretty good es ist ganz gut [. . . gants goot]
price der Preis [price]
priest der Priester [preester]
print *(photo)* ein Abzug [app-tsoog]
printed matter Drucksache [drōōck-zahk-uh]
prison das Gefängnis [gheh-fengnis]
private privat [pree-vaht]
probably wahrscheinlich [vahr-shine-lish]
problem das Problem [prob-laym]
product das Produkt [prodoockt]
profit der Gewinn [gheh-vinn]
promise: do you promise? versprechen Sie es?
[fair-shpreshen zee ess]
   I promise ehrlich! [air-lish]
pronounce: how do you pronounce it? wie
spricht man das aus? [vee shprisht man dass
ōwss]
propeller der Propeller
properly richtig [rik-tik]
property das Eigentum [eye-ghen-toom]
   (land) der Besitz [buh-zits]

prostitute die Prostituierte [prostit-oo-*eer*-tuh]
protect schützen [shootsen]
Protestant evangelisch [ay-van-*gay*-lish]
proud stolz [shtolts]
prove: I can prove it ich kann es beweisen [ish kann ess buh-*vise*-en]
public: the public die Öffentlichkeit [urrfent-lish-kite]
    public convenience öffentliche Toilette [urrfent-lish-uh twa-lettuh]
» *TRAVEL TIP: there are not very many public conveniences in Germany; try the railway station; the attitude towards using cafe etc is the same as in Britain*
    public holiday gesetzlicher Feiertag [gheh-zets-lisher fire-tahg]
» *TRAVEL TIP: public holidays are:*
    New Year's Day *Neujahr*
    Good Friday *Karfreitag*
    Easter Monday *Ostermontag*
    May Day *Erster Mai*
    Ascension Day *Christi Himmelfahrt*
    Whit Monday *Pfingstmontag*
    National Unity Day *Tag der deutschen Einheit (17th June)*
    Day of Prayer and Repentance *Buß- und Bettag (mid Nov)*
    Christmas Day *1. (erster) Weihnachtsfeiertag*
    Boxing Day *2. (zweiter) Weihnachtsfeiertag;* in the mainly Catholic parts there is also:
    Epiphany *Dreikönige*
    Corpus Christi *Fronleichnam*
    Assumption *Mariä Himmelfahrt*
pudding der Pudding
    (dessert) der Nachtisch [nah*k*tish]
pull *(verb)* ziehen [tsee-en]; **he pulled out in front of me** er ist vor mir ausgeschert [air isst for meer owss-gheh-shayrt]
pump die Pumpe [poom-puh]
punctual pünktlich [poonkt-lish]
puncture die Reifenpanne [rye-fen-pan-uh]

pure rein [rine]
purple lila [lee-lah]
purse das Portemonnaie [port-mon-ay]
push *(verb)* schieben [sheeben]
  push-chair der Sportwagen
  [shport-vah-ghen]
put: where can I put ...? wo kann ich ...
  hintun? [voh kann ish ... hintoon]
  where have you put it? wo haben Sie es
  hingetan? [voh hah-ben zee es hin-gheh-tahn]
pyjamas der Schlafanzug [shlahf-an-tsoog]
quality die Qualität [kval-ee-tayt]
quarantine die Quarantäne [kvar-an-tayn-uh]
quarter ein Viertel [feer-tel]
  a quarter of an hour eine Viertelstunde
  [ine-uh feer-tel shtoon-duh]
quay der Kai [kye]
question die Frage [frah-guh]
queue *(noun)* die Schlange [shlang-uh]
» *TRAVEL TIP: orderly queueing, as in Britain, is
not one of the most German habits*
quick schnell [shnel]
  that was quick das ging schnell
quiet ruhig [roo-ik]; *(not noisy)* still [shtill]
quite ganz [gants]
  quite a lot ziemlich viel [tseem-lish feel]
race das Rennen
radiator der Kühler [kooler]
  (heater) der Heizkörper [hites-kurr-per]
radio das Radio [rah-dee-oh]
Radweg cycle path
rail: by rail per Bahn [pair ...]
rain der Regen [ray-ghen]
  it's raining es regnet [ess rayg-net]
  raincoat der Regenmantel
rally *(car)* die Rallye
rape die Vergewaltigung [fair-gheh-val-tigoong]
rare selten [z-]; *(steak)* blutig [bloo-tik]
raspberries Himbeeren [him-bair-en]
rat die Ratte [rat-uh]
rather: I'd rather sit here ich würde lieber

hier sitzen [ish vōōr-duh *lee*-ber heer zitsen]
I'd rather have a . . . ich hätte lieber ein . . .
[ish het-uh *lee*-ber ine]
I'd rather not lieber nicht! [*lee*-ber nisht]
it's rather hot es ist ganz schön heiß [ess isst
gants shurrn hice]
Rauchen verboten no smoking
Raucher smoking compartment
raw roh
razor der Rasierapparat [ra-*zeer*–]
razor blades Rasierklingen
read: you read it lesen Sie es [*lay*-zen zee ess]
something to read etwas zu lesen [et-vass
tsoo . . .]
ready: when will it be ready? wann ist es
fertig [van isst ess *fair*-ti*k*]
I'm not ready yet ich bin noch nicht fertig [ish
bin no*k* nisht . . .]
real *(genuine)* echt [esht]
really wirklich [*veerk*-lish]
rear-view mirror der Rückspiegel
[*rōōck*-shpee-ghel]
reasonable vernünftig [fair-*nōōnf*-ti*k*]
receipt die Quittung [kvit-ong]
can I have a receipt, please? kann ich, bitte,
eine Quittung haben? [kan ish bittuh
ine-uh . . . *hah*-ben]
recently kürzlich [*kōōrts*-lish]
reception *(hotel)* der Empfang
at reception am Empfang
receptionist der Empfangschef
(lady) die Empfangsdame [–dah-muh]
rechts fahren keep right
recipe das Rezept [rets-ept]
recommend: can you recommend . . .?
können Sie . . . empfehlen? [kurrn-en zee . . .
emp-*fay*-len]
record *(music)* die Platte [plat-uh]
red rot [roht]
reduction *(in price)* die Ermäßigung
[air-*ma*ce-ee-g*o*ong]

....

refuse: I refuse ich weigere mich [ish vy-guh-ruh mish]

region das Gebiet [gheh-b*ee*t]
in this region in diesem Gebiet [in dee-zem . . .]

registered: I want to send it registered ich möchte das per Einschreiben schicken [ish murrsh-tuh das pair ine-shryben shicken]

regret das Bedauern [buh-d*ow*ern]
I have no regrets ich bereue nichts [ish buh-r*oy*-uh nix]

relax: I just want to relax ich möchte mich nur entspannen [ish murrsh-tuh mish noor ent-shpannen]
relax! ganz ruhig! [gants roo-i*k*]

remember: don't you remember? wissen Sie das nicht mehr? [vissen zee dass nisht mair]
I'll always remember ich werde es nie vergessen [ish vair-duh ess nee fair-gh*e*ssen]
something to remember you by ein Andenken an dich [ine . . . dish]

rent: can I rent a car/boat/bicycle? kann ich ein Auto/Boot/Fahrrad mieten? [. . . meeten]

repair: can you repair it? können Sie es reparieren? [kurrn-en zee ess rep-a-r*ee*-ren]

repeat: could you repeat that? könnten Sie das wiederholen? [kurrn-ten zee dass veeder-h*o*le-en]

reputation der Ruf [roof]

rescue *(verb)* retten

reservation die Reservierung [rez-air-v*ee*-r*oo*ng]
I want to make a reservation for . . . *(hotel)* ich möchte ein Zimmer für . . . bestellen [ish murrsh-tuh ine tsimmer f*oo*r . . buh-sht*e*llen]
(theatre) ich möchte einen Platz reservieren für . . . [. . . ine-en plats rez-air-v*ee*-ren . . .]

reserve: can I reserve a seat/table? kann ich einen Platz/Tisch reservieren? [kan ish ine-en plats/tish rez-air-v*ee*-ren]

responsible verantwortlich [fair-*a*nt-vort-lish]

....

rest: I've come here for a rest ich bin hier, um
mal auszuspannen [ish bin heer oom mal
ōwss-tsoo-shpannen]

you keep the rest der Rest ist für Sie [. . . isst
foor zee]

restaurant ein Restaurant [–rong]

retail price der Einzelhandelspreis
[ine-tsel-handels-price]

retired pensioniert [pen-zee-oh-neert]

return: a return to . . . eine Rückfahrkarte
nach . . . [rōck-fahr-kartuh nahk]

reverse charge call ein R-Gespräch
[air-gheh-shpraysh]

reverse gear der Rückwärtsgang [rōck-vairts–]

rheumatism der Rheumatismus [roy-ma-
tismooss]

rib eine Rippe [rip-uh]

rice der Reis [rice]

rich reich [rysh] *(food)* schwer [shvair]

ridiculous lächerlich [lesh-er-lish]

right: that's right das stimmt [dass shtimmt]

you're right Sie haben recht [zee hah-ben
resht]

on the right rechts [reshts]

right here genau hier [gheh-nōw heer]

righthand drive rechts gesteuert [reshts
gheh-shtoy-ert]

ring *(on finger)* der Ring

ripe reif [rife]

rip-off: it's a rip-off das ist Wucher! [dass isst
vook-er]

river der Fluß [flōoss]

road die Straße [shtrass-uh]

which is the road to . . .? wo geht es nach . . .?
[voh gayt ess nahk . . .]

roadhog der Verkehrsrowdy [fair-kairs–]

rob: I've been robbed ich bin bestohlen
worden [ish bin buh-shtole-en vorden]

rock der Fels [felz]

whisky on the rocks Whisky mit Eis [. . . ice]

roll *(bread)* ein Brötchen [brurrt-shen]

Roman Catholic (römisch-) katholisch
[(rurr-mish) kat-*o*lish]
romantic romantisch [–tish]
roof das Dach [dah*k*]
room das Zimmer [tsimmer]
  have you got a (single/double) room? haben
  Sie ein (Einzel/Doppel)zimmer [h*a*h-ben zee ine
  (ine-tsel/doppel) . . .]
  for one night/for three nights für eine
  Nacht/für drei Nächte [f*oo*r ine-uh nah*k*t/f*oo*r
  dry neshte]
  YOU MAY THEN HEAR . . .
  mit Bad oder ohne? *with or without bath?*
  tut mir leid, wir sind voll ausgebucht/wir haben
  nichts mehr frei *sorry, we're full*
room service der Zimmerservice [tsimmer-
  serviss]
rope das Seil [zile]
rose die Rose [roh-zuh]
rough rauh [r*ō*w]
roughly ungefähr [*oo*n-gheh-fair]
roulette das Roulett(e)
round *(circular)* rund [r*oo*nt]
roundabout der Kreisverkehr [kr*i*ce-fair-kair]
route die Strecke [shtreck-uh]
  which is the prettiest/fastest route? was ist
  die schönste/schnellste Strecke?
  [. . . shurrn-stuh/shnel-stuh . . .]
rowing boat das Ruderboot [rooder-boht]
rubber der Gummi [g*oo*-mee]
  rubberband ein Gummiband [–bannt]
rubbish der Mist
  (garbage) der Abfall [app-fal]
  rubbish! Quatsch! [kvatsh]
rucksack der Rucksack [r*oo*ck–]
rudder das Ruder [rooder]
rude unhöflich [*oo*n-hurrf-lish]
Ruhetag closed all day
ruin die Ruine [roo-een-uh]
rum ein Rum [r*oo*m]
  rum and coke Cola mit Rum

run: hurry, run! beeil dich, lauf! [buh-ile dish lōwf]

I've run out of petrol/money mir ist das Benzin/Geld ausgegangen [meer isst dass ben-tseen/gelt ōws-gheh-gang-en]

Sackgasse *cul-de-sac*

sad traurig [trōw-ri*k*]

safe sicher [zisher]

will it be safe here? ist es hier sicher? [isst es heer . . .]

is it safe to swim here? kann man hier ohne Gefahr schwimmen? [. . . oh-nuh gheh-fahr shvimmen]

safety die Sicherheit [zisher-hite]

safety pin eine Sicherheitsnadel [–snah-del]

sail segeln [zay-gheln]

can we go sailing? können wir segeln gehen? [kurrn-en veer . . . gay-en]

sailor ein Seemann [zay-man]

(sports) ein Segler [zaygler]

salad ein Salat [zal-aht]

salami die Salami [z–]

sale: is it for sale? kann man das kaufen? [. . . kōw-fen]

salmon der Lachs [lax]

salt das Salz [zalts]

same der-/die-/dasselbe [dair-/dee-/dass-zelbuh]

the same again, please das gleiche noch mal, bitte [dass glysh-uh no*k* mal bittuh]

the same to you (danke) gleichfalls [(dankuh) glysh-falz]

sand der Sand [zannt]

sandal die Sandale [zan-d*a*hl-uh]

sandwich ein Sandwich

sanitary towel die Damenbinde [dah-men-bin-duh]

satisfactory befriedigend [buh-freed-ee-ghent]

Saturday Samstag [zamz-tahg]

sauce die Soße [zoh-suh]

saucepan der Kochtopf [ko*k*-topf]

saucer der Unterteller [ɔonter–]

....

sauna die Sauna [zōw-na]
sausage die Wurst [vœrst]
save *(life)* retten
say: how do you say ... in German? was heißt ... auf Deutsch? [vass hysst ... ōwf doytsh]
> **what did he say?** was hat er gesagt? [vass hat air gheh-zahgt]
scarf der Schal [shahl]
> *(neck scarf)* das Halstuch [halz-took]
> *(headscarf)* das Kopftuch
scenery die Landschaft [lannt-shafft]
schedule der Zeitplan [tsite-plahn]
> **on/behind schedule** pünktlich/verspätet [pōōnkt-lish/fair-shpaytet]
> *(work)* **on schedule** programmgemäß [program-gheh-mace]; **behind schedule** im Verzug [fair-tsœg]
> **scheduled flight** der Linienflug [leen-ee-en-floog]
Schlafwagen sleeper
Schließfächer luggage lockers
Schlußverkauf sale
schnaps ein Schnaps
» *TRAVEL TIP: can be made from practically anything; try North German 'Korn' (grain), Black Forest 'Kirsch' (cherries) or 'Steinhäger' [shtine-hay-gher] (juniper berries)*
school die Schule [shool-uh]
scissors: a pair of scissors eine Schere [ine-uh shay-ruh]
scooter der (Motor)roller
Scot Schotte [shot-uh] *(woman)* Schottin
Scotland Schottland [shott-lannt]
Scottish schottisch [shottish]
scrambled eggs Rührei [rōōr-eye]
scratch der Kratzer
scream *(verb)* schreien [shry-en]
screw die Schraube [shrōw-buh]
> **screwdriver** ein Schraubenzieher [–ben-tsee-er]

....

sea das Meer [mayr]; **by the sea** am Meer
seafood Meeresfrüchte [mayr-es-frōōkt-uh]
search die Suche [zook-uh]
   search party die Suchmannschaft
   [zook-man-shafft]
seasick: I get seasick ich werde seekrank [ish
   vairduh zay–]
seaside: let's go to the seaside fahren wir ans
   Meer! [fahren veer anz mayr]
season die Saison [sez-ong]
   in the high/low season in der Hochsaison/
   Nebensaison [in dair hohk–/nay-ben–]
seasoning das Gewürz [gheh-vōōrts]
seat der (Sitz)platz
   is this somebody's seat? sitzt hier jemand?
   [zitst heer yay-mannt]
   seat belt der Sicherheitsgurt [zisher-
   hites-goort]
seaweed der Tang
second *(adjective)* zweite [tsvy-tuh]
   (time) die Sekunde [zeck-oonduh]
   just a second Moment!
   second class zweite Klasse [. . . klass-uh . . .]
   second hand gebraucht [gheh-browkt]
see sehen [zay-en]
   oh, I see ach so! [ahk zoh]
   have you seen . . . haben Sie . . . gesehen?
   [hah-ben zee . . . gheh-zay-en]
   can I see the room? kann ich mir das Zimmer
   anschauen? [kan ish meer dass tsimmer
   an-show-en]
seem scheinen [shine-en]
   it seems so so sieht es aus [zoh zeet ess ōwss]
seldom selten [zelten]
self: self-service Selbstbedienung [zelpst-
   buh-deen-oong]
sell verkaufen [fair-kōwfen]
send schicken [shicken]
sensitive empfindlich [emp-finnt-lish]
sentimental sentimental
separate getrennt [gheh–]

I'm separated wir leben getrennt [veer *lay*-ben . . .]

can we pay separately? können wir getrennt zahlen? [kurrn-en veer . . . ts*ah*-len]

September September [z–]

serious ernst [airnst]

I'm serious ich meine das ernst [ish my-nuh dass . . .]

this is serious das ist ernst

is it serious, doctor? ist es schlimm? [isst ess shlim]

service: the service was excellent/poor der Service war ausgezeichnet/schlecht [dair serviss vahr ōwss-gheh-tsysh-net/shlessht]

service station die Tankstelle (mit Reparaturwerkstatt) [tank-shtelluh (mit rep-a-rah-*too*r-vairk-shtat)]

serviette eine Serviette [zair-vee-ett-uh]

several mehrere [mair-uh-ruh]

sexy sexy

shade: in the shade im Schatten [. . . shat-en]

shake schütteln [sh*oo*t-eln]

to shake hands die Hand schütteln [dee hannt . . .]

» *TRAVEL TIP: it is normal to shake hands each time you meet someone and when you leave someone*

shallow seicht [zysht]

shame: what a shame wie schade! [vee shah-duh]

shampoo ein Shampoo(n); **shampoo and set** Waschen und Legen [vashen *oo*nt *lay*-ghen]

shandy ein Bier mit Limonade [ine beer mit lee-mo-n*ah*-duh]; *(in South Germany)* ein Radlermaß [ine r*ah*t-ler-mahss]

share *(room)* teilen [tile-en]

(table) gemeinsam nehmen [gheh-m*i*ne-zahm n*a*y-men]

sharp scharf [sharf]

shave rasieren [ra-*zee*-ren]

shaver der Rasierapparat [ra-zeer–]

shaving foam der Rasierschaum [–shōwm]

....

shaving point eine Steckdose für
Rasierapparate [ine-uh sht*eck*-doh-zuh för . . .]
she sie [zee] **she is** sie ist [zee isst]
sheep das Schaf [shahf]
sheet das Leintuch [l*i*ne-took]
shelf das Regal [ray-g*a*hl]
shell die Schale [shah-luh]
  (on beach) die Muschel [m*oo*shel]
  shellfish Meeresfrüchte [mayr-es-fr*oo*sh-tuh]
shelter *(noun)* der Unterstand [*oo*nter-shtannt]
  can we shelter here? können wir hier unter-
  stehen? [kurrn-en veer heer *oo*nter-shtay-en]
sherry ein Sherry
ship das Schiff [shif]
shirt das Hemd [hemmt]
shock *(noun: surprise)* der Schock
  what a shock so ein Schreck! [zoh ine shreck]
  I got an electric shock from the . . . ich habe
  von dem . . . einen Schlag bekommen [ish
  h*a*h-buh fon d*a*ym . . . ine-nen shlahg buh–]
  shock-absorber der Stoßdämpfer [shtohss-
  dem-pfer]
shoe der Schuh [shoo]
» *TRAVEL TIP: shoe sizes:*

UK	4	5	6	7	8	9	10	11
Germany	37	38	39	41	42	43	44	46

shop das Geschäft [gheh-sh*e*fft]
  I've some shopping to do ich muß noch ein
  paar Einkäufe erledigen [ish m*oo*ss no*k* ine par
  *i*ne-koy-fuh air-lay-dig-en]
» *TRAVEL TIP: shops generally open from*
  9.00–18.30; closed Saturday afternoon except
  the first Saturday in the month
shore das Ufer [oofer]
  (sea) der Strand [shtrannt]
short kurz [k*oo*rts]
  I'm three short mir fehlen drei [meer fay-len
  dry]
  short cut eine Abkürzung [ine-uh *a*pp-
  k*öö*rts-*oo*ng]
shorts die Shorts

shoulder die Schulter [shoolter]

shout rufen [roofen]

show: please show me bitte zeigen Sie es mir [bittuh-tsy-ghen zee ess meer]

shower: with shower mit Dusche [mit doosh-uh]

shrimp eine Garnele [gar-nay-luh]

shrink: it's shrunk es ist eingegangen [ess isst ine-gheh-gang-en]

shut *(verb)* schließen [shlee-sen]

when do you shut? wann machen Sie zu? [van mah-ken zee tsoo]

shut up! halt den Mund! [hallt dayn moont]

shy schüchtern [shoosh-tern]

sick krank

I feel sick mir ist schlecht [meer isst shlesht]

he's been sick er hat gebrochen [air hat gheh-brok-en]

side die Seite [zy-tuh]

side light das Standlicht [shtannt-lisht]

side street die Nebenstraße [nay-ben-shtrahss-uh]

by the side of the road an der Straße

sight: out of sight außer Sicht [owsser zisht]

the sights of . . . die Sehenswürdigkeiten von [zay-enz-voord-ik-kite-en fon]

sightseeing tour eine Rundreise [roont-ry-zuh] *(of town)* eine Stadtrundfahrt [shtat-roont-fahrt]

sign *(notice)* das Schild [shilt]

signal: he didn't signal er hat kein Zeichen gegeben [air hat kine tsyshen gheh-gay-ben]

signature die Unterschrift [oonter-shrift]

silencer der Schalldämpfer [shall-dem-pfer]

silk die Seide [zy-duh]

silly dumm [doomm]

silver das Silber [zilber]

similar ähnlich [ayn-lish]

simple einfach [ine-fahk]

since: since last week seit letzter Woche [zite lets-ter vock-uh]; *(because)* weil [vile]

sincere aufrichtig [ōwf-ri*k*-ti*k*]
  yours sincerely mit freundlichen Grüßen
sing singen [zing-en]
single: single room ein Einzelzimmer [ine-tsel-tsimmer]
  I'm single ich bin ledig [ish bin l*a*y-di*k*]
  a single/two singles to . . . einmal einfach/zweimal einfach nach . . . [ine-mal ine-fah*k*/tsvy-m*a*l ine-fah*k* nah*k*]
sink: it sank es ist gesunken [ess isst gheh-z*oo*nken]
sir Herr . . .
sister: my sister meine Schwester [mine-uh shvester]
sit: can I sit here? kann ich mich hierher setzen? [kan ish mish heer-hair zetsen]
size die Größe [grurr-suh]
ski *(noun)* der Ski [shee]; *(verb)* skifahren
  skiing das Skifahren
  ski boots die Skistiefel [–shteefel]
  ski lift der Skilift
  ski pants die Skihose [–hoh-zuh]
  ski pole der Skistock [–shtock]
  ski slope/run der Skihang/die Skipiste
  ski wax das Skiwachs [–vax]
skid schleudern [shl*o*y-dern]
skin die Haut [h*ō*wt]
skirt der Rock
sky der Himmel
sledge der Schlitten [sh–]
sleep: I can't sleep ich kann nicht schlafen [ish kan nisht shl*a*h-fen]
  sleeper *(rail)* der Schlafwagen [shl*a*hf-vah-ghen]
  sleeping bag der Schlafsack
  sleeping pill die Schlaftablette [–lettuh]
  YOU MAY HEAR . . .
  haben Sie gut geschlafen? *did you sleep well?*
sleeve der Ärmel [*air*-mel]
slide *(phot)* das Dia [d*ee*-ah]
slippery glatt

slow langsam [lang-zahm]
   could you speak a little slower? könnten Sie
   etwas langsamer sprechen? [kurrn-ten zee et-
   vass lang-zahmer shpreshen]
small klein [kline]
   small change das Kleingeld [–gelt]
smell: there's a funny smell hier riecht es
   komisch [heer reekt ess koh-mish]
   it smells es stinkt [ess shtinkt]
smile *(verb)* lächeln [lesh-eln]
smoke *(noun)* der Rauch [rowk]
   do you smoke? rauchen Sie? [rowken zee]
   can I smoke? darf ich rauchen?
smooth glatt
snack: can we just have a snack? können wir
   einen Imbiß bekommen? [kurrn-en veer ine-en
   im-biss buh-kommen]
» *TRAVEL TIP: you will find plenty of indoor and*
   outdoor snackbars called 'Schnellimbiß' or
   'Imbißstube' which sell sausages, chips etc
snow *(noun)* der Schnee [shnay]
   it's snowing es schneit [ess shnite]
» *TRAVEL TIP: snow chains (Schneeketten) can be*
   hired from ADAC depots
so so [zoh]
   not so much nicht so viel [nisht zoh feel]
   so so so la la
soap die Seife [zy-fuh]; **soap powder** das
   Seifenpulver [zy-fen-poolver]
sober nüchtern [nooshtern]
sock die Socke [zock-uh]
soda(water) das Soda(wasser)
soft drink ein alkoholfreies Getränk
   [al-koh-hole-fry-es gheh-trenk]
Sofortreinigung *fast service dry-cleaner's*
sole die Sohle [zoh-luh]
   could you put new soles on these? könnten
   Sie diese hier neu besohlen? [kurrn-ten zee
   dee-zuh heer noy buh-zoh-len]
   YOU MAY THEN HEAR . . .
   Leder- oder Gummisohle? *leather or rubber?*

some: some people einige Leute [ine-ig-uh loy-tuh]
  can I have some? kann ich ein wenig bekommen? [kan ish ine v*a*y-ni*k* buh-kommen]
  can I have some grapes/some bread? kann ich ein paar Trauben/etwas Brot haben? [. . . ine par trōw-ben/et-vass broht . . .]
  can I have some more? kann ich noch ein wenig bekommen? [. . . no*k* ine v*a*y-ni*k* . . .]
  that's some drink! das ist vielleicht ein Getränk! [dass isst fee-lysht ine geh-tr*e*nk]
somebody jemand [y*a*y-mannt]
something etwas [et-vass]
sometime irgendwann [eer-ghent-van]
sometimes manchmal [mansh-mal]
somewhere irgendwo [eer-ghent-voh]
son: my son mein Sohn [mine zohn]
song das Lied [leet]
soon bald [balt]; **as soon as possible** so bald wie möglich [zoh balt vee murr-glish]
  sooner früher [frōo-er]
sore: it's sore es tut weh [ess toot vay]
  sore throat das Halsweh [halz-vay]
sorry: (I'm) sorry Entschuldigung! [ent-shool-dig*oo*ng]
sort: this sort diese Art [dee-zuh art]
  will you sort it out? können Sie das in Ordnung bringen? [kurrn-en zee dass in ort-n*oo*ng . . .]
  what sort of? was für ein? [vass fōor ine]
soup die Suppe [z*oo*pp-uh]
sour sauer [zōw-er]
south der Süden [z*oo*-den]
South Africa Südafrika [zōod-*a*f-ree-ka]
South African südafrikanisch [zōod-af-ree-k*a*hn-ish] *(person)* Südafrikaner *(woman)* Südafrikanerin
souvenir ein Souvenir
spade ein Spaten [shpaht-en]
spanner ein Schraubenschlüssel [shrōw-ben-shlōosel]

spare: spare part das Ersatzteil [air-zats-tile]
  spare wheel das Ersatzrad [–raht]
spark(ing) plug die Zündkerze [tsoont-kairtsuh]
speak: do you speak English? sprechen Sie
  Englisch? [shpreshen zee eng-glish]
  I don't speak . . . ich kann kein . . . [ish kan
  kine]
special besonderer [buh-zon-der-ruh]
specialist der Fachmann [fahk-man]
specially besonders [buh-zonders]
spectacles die Brille [brill-uh]
speed die Geschwindigkeit [geh-shvin-dik-
  kite]
  he was speeding er ist zu schnell gefahren
  [air isst tsoo shnell geh-fahren]
  speed limit die Geschwindigkeitsbegrenzung
  [–sbuh-grents-oong]
  speedometer der Tachometer [tak-o-may-ter]
Speisewagen *dining car*
spend *(money)* ausgeben [owss-gay-ben]
spice das Gewürz [geh-voorts]
  is it spicy? ist es stark gewürzt? [. . .
  shtark . . .]
spider die Spinne [shpin-uh]
spirits die Spirituosen [shpirit-oo-ozen]
spoon der Löffel [lurr-fel]
sprain: I've sprained it ich habe es mir
  verstaucht [ish hah-buh ess meer fair-shtowkt]
Sprechstunden *surgery hours*
spring die Feder [fay-der]
  (water) die Quelle [kvel-uh]
  (season) der Frühling [froo-ling]
square *(in town)* der Platz
  2 square metres 2 Quadratmeter [tsvy
  kvad-raht-may-ter]
stairs die Treppe [trep-uh]
stale altbacken
stalls das Parkett
stamp eine Briefmarke [breef-mark-uh]
  two stamps for England zwei Briefmarken
  nach England [tsvy . . . nahk eng-glannt]

....

stand stehen [shtay-en]
  (noun: at fair) der Stand [shtannt]
standard *(adjective)* normal [nor-mahl]
stand-by *(ticket)* Standby-
star der Stern [shtairn]
starboard Steuerbord [shtoy-er-bort]
start der Anfang; *(of race)* der Start [shtart]
  my car won't start mein Auto springt nicht
  an [mine ōwtoh shpringt nisht an]
  when does it start? wann fängt es an? [van
  fengt ess an]
starter *(car)* der Starter [shtarter]
starving: I'm starving ich habe einen
  Riesenhunger [ish hah-buh ine-en ree-zen-
  hoong-er]
station der Bahnhof [bahn-hohff]
statue die Statue [shtaht-oo-uh]
stay *(noun)* der Aufenthalt [ōwf-ent-hallt]
  we enjoyed our stay es hat uns hier gut
  gefallen [ess hat oonts heer goot gheh-fal-en]
  I'm staying at . . . ich wohne im . . . [ish
  voh-nuh im]
  stay there bleiben Sie dort [bly-ben zee . . .]
steak ein Steak [sht–]
  YOU MAY HEAR...
  wie möchten Sie Ihr Steak gebraten haben? –
  ganz durch, halb durch oder blutig? [. . . gants
  doorsh, halp doorsh oh-der-blootik]
  how would you like your steak done? well done,
  medium or rare?
steep steil [shtile]
steering *(car)* die Lenkung [lenk-oong]
steering wheel das Steuerrad [shtoy-er-raht]
Stehplätze *standing room*
step *(noun)* die Stufe [shtoo-fuh]
stereo das Stereo
  (unit) die Stereoanlage [ster-ay-o-an-lah-guh]
sterling Sterling
stewardess die Stewardeß
sticky klebrig [klay-brik]
sticking plaster das (Heft)pflaster [–pflass-ter]

....

stiff steif [shtife]

still : keep still bewegen Sie sich nicht
[buh-vay-ghen zee zish nisht]

I'm still here ich bin immer noch da [. . .
nok . . .]

stink *(noun)* der Gestank [gheh-shtank]

stolen: my wallet's been stolen man hat mir
meine Brieftasche gestohlen [man hat meer
mine-uh breef-tash-uh gheh-shtole-en]

stomach der Magen [mah-ghen]

I've got stomach-ache ich habe
Magenschmerzen [ish hah-buh mah-ghen-
shmairtsen]

**have you got something for an upset
stomach?** haben Sie etwas gegen
Magenbeschwerden? [hah-ben zee et-vass
gay-ghen mah-ghen-buh-shvairden]

stone der Stein [shtine]

» *TRAVEL TIP: 1 stone = 6.35 kilos*

stop: stop! halt! [hallt]

stop-over die Zwischenstation
[tsvishen-shtats-ee-ohn]

do you stop near . . .? halten Sie in der Nähe
von . . .? [hal-ten zee in dair nay-uh fon]

storm der Sturm [shtoorm]

. . . ist strafbar . . . is an offence

straight gerade [gheh-rah-duh]

go straight on gehen Sie geradeaus [gay-en
zee gheh-rah-duh-ōwss]

straight away sofort [zoh-fort]

straight whisky Whisky pur [. . . poor]

strange fremd [fremmt]

(odd) seltsam [zelt-zahm]

stranger der Fremde [frem-duh]

I'm a stranger here ich bin fremd hier [ish bin
fremmt heer]

strawberries Erdbeeren [airt-bair-en]

street die Straße [shtrahss-uh]

string: have you got any string? haben Sie
Schnur? [hah-ben zee shnoor]

stroke: he's had a stroke er hat einen

Schlag(anfall) bekommen [air hat ine-en
shlahg-an-fal buh-kommen]
strong stark [shtark]
student der Student [shtoo-dent]; *(girl)* die
Studentin
stung: I've been stung ich bin gestochen
worden [ish bin gheh-shtoken vorden]
stupid dumm [dœmm]
such: such a lot so viel [zoh feel]
suddenly plötzlich [plurrts-lish]
sugar der Zucker [tsœcker]
suit *(man's)* der Anzug [an-tsoog]
(woman's) das Kostüm [kostoom]
suitcase der Koffer
suitable passend [pas-ent]
summer der Sommer [zommer]
sun die Sonne [zonnuh]
  in the sun in der Sonne
  out of the sun im Schatten [shat-en]
  sunbathe sonnenbaden [zonnen-bah-den]
  sunburn der Sonnenbrand [–brannt]
  sunglasses die Sonnenbrille [–brill-uh]
  suntan lotion das Sonnenöl [–urrl]
Sunday Sonntag [zonn-tahg]
supermarket der Supermarkt [zooper–]
supper das Abendessen [ah-bent–]
sure: I'm not sure ich bin nicht sicher [ish bin
nisht zisher] **sure!** sicher!
  are you sure? sind Sie sicher? [zinnt zee . . .]
surname der Zuname [tsoo-nah-muh]
swearword der Fluch [flook]
sweat *(verb)* schwitzen [shvitsen]
sweet süß [zooss]
  (dessert) der Nachtisch [nahk-tish]
sweets die Süßigkeiten [zooss-ik-kite-en]
swerve: I had to swerve ich mußte
ausschwenken [ish mœss-tuh ōwss-shvenken]
swim: I'm going for a swim ich gehe
schwimmen [ish gay-uh shvimmen]
  swimming costume der Badeanzug [bah-
duh-an-tsoog]

swimming pool das Schwimmbad [shv*i*mm-baht]

Swiss Schweizer [shv*y*-tser]
(person) Schweizer; *(woman)* Schweizerin

switch *(noun)* der Schalter [sh*a*ll-ter]
  to switch on/off anschalten/abschalten [*a*n-shall-ten /*a*pp–]

Switzerland die Schweiz [shvites]
  in Switzerland in der Schweiz

table ein Tisch [tish]
  a table for 4 ein Tisch für vier [. . . f$\overline{oo}$r . . .]
  table wine Tafelwein [t*a*h-fel-vine]

take nehmen [n*a*y-men]
  can I take this with me? kann ich das mitnehmen?
  will you take me to the airport? bringen Sie mich zum Flughafen? [. . . zee mish ts$\overline{oo}$m floog-hah-fen]
  how long will it take? wie lange dauert es? [vee lang-uh d$\overline{o}$wert ess]
  somebody has taken my bags jemand hat mein Gepäck mitgenommen [yay-mannt hat mine gheh-p*e*ck mit-gheh-nommen]
  can I take you out tonight? kann ich Sie für heute abend einladen? [kan ish zee f$\overline{oo}$r hoy-tuh ah-bent *i*ne-lah-den]

talcum powder der (Körper)puder [(kurr-per)pooder]

talk *(verb)* sprechen [shpreshen]

tall groß [grohss]

tampons die Tampons

tan die Bräune [bro*y*-nuh]

tank *(of car)* der Tank

tap der Hahn

tape das Tonband [t*o*hn-bannt]

tape-recorder das Tonbandgerät [–gheh-rayt]

tariff der Tarif [tah-r*ee*f]
  (in hotels) die Preisliste [price-list-uh]

taste *(noun)* der Geschmack [gheh-shm*a*ck]
  can I taste it? kann ich es versuchen? [kan ish ess fair-z*ook*en]

....

it tastes horrible/very nice das schmeckt
fürchterlich/sehr gut [dass shmeckt
fo͞orsh-terlish/zair goot]

taxi ein Taxi
will you get me a taxi? rufen Sie mir, bitte,
ein Taxi! [roofen zee meer bittuh . . .]
where can I get a taxi? wo bekomme ich ein
Taxi? [voh buh-kommuh ish . . .]
taxi-driver der Taxifahrer

tea der Tee [tay]
could I have a cup/pot of tea? könnte ich
eine Tasse/ein Kännchen Tee haben?
[kurrn-tuh ish ine-uh tass-uh/ine ken-shen tay
hah-ben]
YOU MAY THEN HEAR . . .
mit Zitrone? *with lemon?*
no, with milk, please nein, mit Milch, bitte
[nine mit milsh bittuh]

teach: could you teach me? könnten Sie mir
das beibringen? [kurrn-ten zee meer dass
by-bringen]
could you teach me German? könnten Sie
mir Deutsch beibringen? [. . . doytsh . . .]

teacher der Lehrer [lair-uh]
(woman) die Lehrerin

telegram ein Telegramm
I want to send a telegram ich möchte ein
Telegramm schicken [ish murrsh-tuh . . .]

telephone *(noun)* das Telefon
can I make a phone-call? kann ich hier
telefonieren? [. . . heer tele-foneer-en]
can I speak to . . .? kann ich . . . sprechen?
[. . . spreshen]
could you get the number for me? könnten
Sie die Nummer für mich wählen? [kurrnten
zee dee noomer fo͞or mish vay-len]
telephone directory das Telefonbuch [–book]

» *TRAVEL TIP: lift receiver, money in, dial; unused
coins returned; for international calls look for
boxes with green disc with 'Ausland' or
'International'; code for UK is 0044 and drop*

first 0 of UK area code
YOU MAY HEAR ...
kein Anschluß unter dieser Nummer *number not in use*
bitte warten *please wait*

television das Fernsehen [fairn-zay-en]
I'd like to watch television ich möchte gerne fernsehen [ish murrsh-tuh gairn-uh ...]

tell: could you tell me where ...? könnten Sie mir sagen, wo ...? [kurrn-ten zee meer zah-ghen voh]

temperature die Temperatur [–toor]
he's got a temperature er hat Fieber [air hat feeber]

tennis Tennis; **tennis court** der Tennisplatz
tennis racket der Tennisschläger [–shlay-gher]; **tennis ball** der Tennisball [–bal]

tent das Zelt [tselt]

terminus die Endstation [ent-shtats-ee-ohn]

terrible schrecklich [shrecklish]

terrific sagenhaft [zah-ghen-haft]

than als [alts]; **bigger/older than ...** größer/älter als ... [grurrser/elter ...]

thanks, thank you danke(schön) [dank-uh(shurrn)]
thank you very much vielen Dank [feelen ...]
thank you for your help vielen Dank für Ihre Hilfe [... foor eer-uh hilf-uh]
YOU MAY THEN HEAR ...
bitteschön, bitte sehr *you're welcome*

that dieser, diese, dieses [deez-er, deez-uh, deez-es]
that man/that table der Mann (dort)/der Tisch (dort)
I'd like that one ich möchte das da [ish murrsh-tuh ...]
how do you say that? wie spricht man das aus? [vee shprisht man dass ōwss]
I think that ... ich glaube, daß ... [ish glōw-buh dass]

....

the der, die, das; *(plural)* die

theatre das Theater [tay-*a*h-ter]

their ihr [eer]; **it's their bag/it's theirs** das ist ihre Tasche/das ist ihre [. . . eer-uh . . .]

them sie [zee]
  with them mit ihnen [. . . een-en]

then dann

there dort
  how do I get there? wie komme ich dahin? [vee komm-uh ish dah-hin]
  is there/are there? gibt es? [gheept ess]
  there is/there are es gibt
  there you are *(giving something)* hier, bitte! [heer bittuh]

these diese [deez-uh]

they sie [zee]; **they are** sie sind [zee zinnt]

thick dick *(stupid)* dumm [d*oo*mm]

thief der Dieb [deep]

thigh der Schenkel [sh–]

thin dünn [d*oo*nn]

thing das Ding
  I've lost all my things ich habe all meine Sachen verloren [ish hah-buh al mine-uh zah-*k*en fair-lor-ren]

think denken
  I'll think it over ich werde es mir überlegen [ish vair-duh ess meer *oo*ber-l*a*y-ghen]
  I think so/I don't think so ich denke schon/ich denke nicht [ish denk-uh shohn . . .]

third *(adjective)* dritte [drit-uh]

thirsty: I'm thirsty ich habe Durst [ish h*a*h-buh d*oo*rst]

this dieser, diese, dieses [deez-er, deez-uh, deez-es]
  can I have this one? kann ich das haben? [. . . dass h*a*h-ben]
  this is my wife/this is Mr . . . (das ist) meine Frau/(das ist) Herr . . . [mine-uh fr*o*w . . .]
  is this . . .? ist das . . .?

those diese (da) [deez-uh (dah)]
  those people diese Leute (da) [. . . loy-tuh . . .]

....

thread *(noun)* der Faden [fah-den]

three drei [dry]

throat der Hals [halz]

throttle *(motorbike, boat)* der Gashebel [gahss-hay-bel]

through durch [dœrsh]

throw *(verb)* werfen [vair-fen]

thumb der Daumen [dōw-men]

thunder *(noun)* der Donner
  thunderstorm ein Gewitter [gheh-vitter]

Thursday Donnerstag [donners-tahg]

ticket *(train)* die Fahrkarte [–kar-tuh]
  (bus) der Fahrschein [–shine]
  (plane) das Ticket
  (cinema) die Eintrittskarte [ine-trits-kar-tuh]
  (cloakroom) die Garderobenmarke
  [gar-duh-roh-ben-mark-uh]
» *TRAVEL TIP: see* **bus**

tie *(necktie)* die Krawatte [krav-at-uh]

Tiefgarage underground parking

tight *(clothes)* eng
  they're too tight sie sind zu eng [zee zinnt tsoo . . .]

tights die Strumpfhose [shtrœmpf-hoh-zuh]

time die Zeit [tsite]
  what's the time? wie spät ist es? [vee shpayt isst ess]
  I haven't got time ich habe keine Zeit [ish hah-buh kine-uh . . .]
  for the time being vorläufig [for-loy-fik]
  this time/last time/next time dieses Mal/letztes Mal/nächstes Mal [deez-es mahl . . .]
  3 times dreimal [dry-mahl]
  have a good time! viel Vergnügen! [feel fair-guh-nōō-ghen]

timetable *(travel)* der Fahrplan [–plahn]
» *TRAVEL TIP: how to tell the time*
  it's one o'clock es ist ein Uhr [. . . ine oor]
  it's 2/3/4/5/6 o'clock es ist zwei/drei/vier/fünf/sechs Uhr [tsvy/dry/feer/fōōnf/zex oor]

....

it's 5/10/20/25 past 7 est ist fünf/zehn/zwanzig/
fünfundzwanzig (Minuten) nach sieben
[fōōnf/tsayn/ tsvan-tsik/fōōnf-ōōnt-tsvan-tsik
nahk zeeben]

it's quarter past 8/8.15 es ist Viertel nach
acht/acht Uhr fünfzehn [feertel nahk ahkt/ahkt
oor fōōnf-tsayn]

it's half past 9/9.30 es ist halb zehn/neun Uhr
dreißig [halp tsayn/noyn oor dry-sik]

it's 25/20 to ten es ist fünf/zehn nach halb zehn
[fōōnf/tsayn nahk halp tsayn]

it's quarter to eleven es ist Viertel vor elf
[feertel for elf]

it's 10/5 to eleven es ist zehn/fünf (Minuten)
vor elf [tsayn/fōōnf for elf]

it's twelve o'clock es ist zwölf (Uhr) [tsvurrlf]
at . . . um . . . [ōōm]

» *TRAVEL TIP: notice that in German half past nine
etc is said as 'half ten'!*

tin *(can)* die Dose [doh-zuh]
 tin-opener der Dosenöffner [doh-zen-urrf-ner]
tip *(noun)* das Trinkgeld [–gelt]
 is the tip included? ist das inklusive
 Bedienung? [isst dass in-kloo-zee-vuh buh-dee-
 nōōng]

» *TRAVEL TIP: tip same people as in UK; also
customary to tip in pubs*

tired müde [mōō-duh]
 I'm tired ich bin müde [ish . . .]
tissues Papiertaschentücher [pa-peer-tashen-
 tōōk-er]
to: to England nach England [nahk . . .]
toast der Toast
tobacco der Tabak
tobacconist's der Tabakwarenladen [–vah-
 ren-lah-den]
today heute [hoy-tuh]
toe die Zehe [tsay-uh]
together zusammen [tsoo-zammen]
 we're together wir sind zusammen

....

can we pay all together? können wir alles zusammen bezahlen? [kurrn-en veer al-less . . . buh-tsah-len]

toilet die Toilette [twa-lettuh]
where are the toilets? wo sind die Toiletten? [voh zinnt dee . . .]
I have to go to the toilet ich muß auf die Toilette [ish mœss ōwf dee . . .]
there's no toilet paper es ist kein Toilettenpapier da [. . . kine –pa-peer dah]
» *TRAVEL TIP: see public conveniences*

tomato die Tomate [tomah-tuh]
tomato juice der Tomatensaft [–zaft]
tomato ketchup das (Tomaten)ketchup

tomorrow morgen [mor-ghen]
tomorrow morning/tomorrow afternoon/ tomorrow evening morgen früh/morgen nachmittag/morgen abend [. . . frō]
the day after tomorrow übermorgen [ōober–]
see you tomorrow bis morgen

ton die Tonne [tonn-uh]
» *TRAVEL TIP: 1 ton = 1,016 kilos*

tongue die Zunge [tsoong-uh]
tonic(water) das Tonic(water)
tonight heute abend [hoy-tuh ah-bent]
tonne die Tonne [tonn-uh]
» *TRAVEL TIP: 1 tonne = 1000 kilos = metric ton*

tonsils die Mandeln
tonsillitis die Mandelentzündung [–ent-tsōōn-doong]

too zu [tsoo] *(also)* auch [ōwk]
that's too much das ist zuviel [dass isst tsoo-feel]

tool das Werkzeug [vairk-tsoyg]

tooth der Zahn [tsahn]
I've got toothache ich habe Zahnweh [ish hah-buh –vay]
toothbrush die Zahnbürste [–bōorst-uh]
toothpaste die Zahnpasta

top: on top of . . . auf [ōwf]
on the top floor im obersten Stock

at the top oben
torch eine Taschenlampe [tashen-lamp-uh]
total *(noun)* die Endsumme [ent-zoom-uh]
tough *(meat)* zäh [tsay]
tour *(of area)* eine Rundreise [roont-ry-zuh]
   (of town) ein Rundfahrt
   (of castle) ein Rundgang
   we'd like to go on a tour of . . . wir möchten
   gern eine Reise/eine Rundfahrt/einen
   Rundgang durch . . . machen [veer murrsh-ten
   gairn . . .]
   we're touring around wir reisen herum [veer
   ry-zen hair-oom]
tourist der Tourist; **I'm only a tourist** ich bin
   fremd hier [ish bin fremmt heer]
tourist office das Fremdenverkehrsbüro
   [frem-den-fair-kairs-boo-roh]
tow *(verb)* abschleppen [app-shleppen]
   can you give me a tow? könnten Sie mich
   abschleppen? [kurrn-ten zee mish . . .]
   towrope das Abschleppseil [–zile]
towards gegen [gay-ghen]
   he was coming straight towards me er kam
   geradewegs auf mich zu [air kahm gheh-rah-
   duh-veggs owf mish tsoo]
towel das Handtuch [hant-took]
town die Stadt [shtat]; **in town** in der Stadt
   would you take me into town? würden Sie
   mich in die Stadt bringen? [voorden zee . . .]
traditional traditionell [tradi-tsee-oh-nel]
   a traditional German meal ein echt
   deutsches Essen [ine esht doytshes . . .]
traffic der Verkehr [fair-kair]
   traffic lights die Ampel
train der Zug [tsoog]
» *TRAVEL TIP: efficient and punctual; if you travel
   Intercity buy your 'Zuschlag' [tsoo-shlahg]
   (surcharge ticket) first*
   YOU MAY HEAR . . .
   noch jemand zugestiegen? *any more tickets,
   please?*

tranquillizers Beruhigungsmittel [buh-roo-igoongs–]

translate übersetzen [ōober-*zet*-sen]
  would you translate that for me? würden Sie das für mich übersetzen? [vōorden zee dass fōor mish . . .]

transmission *(of car)* das Getriebe [gheh-*tree*-buh]

travel agent's das Reisebüro [ry-zuh-bōō-roh]

traveller's cheque der Travellerscheck

tree der Baum [bōwm]

tremendous enorm [ay-*n*orm]

trip *(noun)* die Reise [ry-zuh]
  (outing) der Ausflug [ōwss-floog]
  we want to go on a trip to . . . wir möchten nach . . . fahren [veer murrsh-ten nah*k* . . .]

trouble die Schwierigkeiten [shv*ee*-rik-kite-en]
  I'm having trouble with . . . ich habe Schwierigkeiten mit . . . [ish h*a*h-buh . . .]

trousers die Hose [h*o*h-zuh]

true wahr [vahr]; **it's not true** das ist nicht wahr [dass isst nisht . . .]

trunks *(swimming)* die Badehose [b*a*h-duh-hoh-zuh]

trust: I trust you ich vertraue Ihnen [ish fair-tr*ō*w-uh een-en]

try *(verb)* versuchen [fair-z*ook*-en]
  can I try it on? kann ich es anprobieren? [kan ish ess *a*n-proh-bee-ren]

T-shirt das T-shirt

Tuesday Dienstag [deenz-tahg]

tunnel der Tunnel

turn: where do we turn off? wo biegen wir ab? [voh bee-ghen veer app]
  he turned without indicating er bog ab, ohne Zeichen zu geben [air bohg app oh-nuh tsy-shen tsoo gay-ben]

twice zweimal [tsvy-mal]
  twice as much doppelt soviel [. . . zoh-feel]

twin beds zwei (Einzel)betten [tsvy (ine-tsel)–]

two zwei [tsvy]

....

typewriter die Schreibmaschine [shripe-mash-ee-nuh]

typical typisch [tōō-pish]

tyre der Reifen [ry-fen]

  I need a new tyre ich brauche einen neuen Reifen [ish brōwk-uh ine-en noy-en . . .]

» *TRAVEL TIP: tyre pressures*

lb/sq in	18	20	22	24	26	28	30
kg/sq cm	1.3	1.4	1.5	1.7	1.8	2	2.1

U-Bahn underground

ugly häßlich [hess-lish]

ulcer das Geschwür [gheh-shvōōr]

Ulster Ulster

umbrella der Schirm [sheerm]

Umleitung diversion

uncle: my uncle mein Onkel

uncomfortable unbequem [ŏŏn-buh-kvaym]

unconscious bewußtlos [buh-vŏŏst-lohs]

under unter [ŏŏnter]

underdone *(not cooked)* nicht gar [nisht . . .]

underground *(rail)* die Untergrundbahn, U-Bahn [ŏŏnter-grŏŏnt-bahn, oo-bahn]

understand: I understand ich verstehe [ish fair-shtay-uh]

  I don't understand das verstehe ich nicht

  do you understand? verstehen Sie? [fair-shtay-en zee]

undo aufmachen [ōwf-mah-ken]

unfriendly unfreundlich [ŏŏn-froynt-lish]

unhappy unglücklich [ŏŏn-glŏŏck-lish]

United States die Vereinigten Staaten [dee fair-ine-ik-ten shtah-ten]

unlock aufschließen [ōwf-shlee-sen]

until bis

  not until Tuesday nicht vor Dienstag [nisht for . . .]

unusual ungewöhnlich [ŏŏn-gheh-vurrn-lish]

up: up in the mountains oben in den Bergen

  he's not up yet er ist noch nicht auf [air isst nok nisht ōwf]

  what's up? was ist los? [vass isst lohs]

....

upside-down verkehrt herum [fair-ka*i*rt hair-*oo*m]

upstairs oben

urgent dringend [dring-ent]

us uns [*oo*nts]; **it's us** wir sind's [veer zinnts]

use: can I use . . . ? kann ich . . . benutzen? [kan ish buh-n*oo*t-sen]

useful nützlich [n*oo*ts-lish]

usual(ly) gewöhnlich [gheh-v*u*rrn-lish]

as usual wie gewöhnlich [vee . . .]

U-turn die Wende [ven-duh]

vacancy ein (freies) Zimmer

do you have any vacancies? haben Sie noch Zimmer frei? [h*a*h-ben zee n*o*k tsimmer fry]

vacate *(room)* räumen [roy-men]

vaccination die Impfung [imp-f*oo*ng]

vacuum flask die Thermosflasche [tairmos-flash-uh]

valid gültig [g*oo*lti*k*]; **how long is it valid for?** wie lange gilt es? [vee lang-uh ghilt ess]

valley das Tal [tahl]

valuable wertvoll [vairt-fol]

value *(noun)* der Wert [vairt]

valve das Ventil [ven-t*ee*l]

van der Kombi

(delivery) der Lieferwagen [*l*eefer-vah-ghen]

vanilla Vanille [van-*ee*-luh]

varicose veins die Krampfadern [–ah-dern]

veal das Kalbfleisch [kalp-flysh]

vegetables Gemüse [gheh-m*oo*-zuh]

vegetarian *(noun)* ein Vegetarier [vay-gheh-t*a*r-ee-er]

ventilator der Ventilator [–*l*ah-tor]

verboten *forbidden*

very sehr [zair]; **very much** sehr

via über [*oo*ber]

village das Dorf

vine die Rebe [ray-buh]

vinegar der Essig [–i*k*]

vineyard der Weinberg [v*i*ne-bairk]

vintage der Jahrgang [yahr–]

....

violent heftig [–i*k*]
visa ein Visum [vee-z∞m]
visibility die Sicht [zisht]
visit *(verb)* besuchen [buh-zoo*k*-en]
vodka der Wodka [v–]
voice die Stimme [shtim-uh]
voltage die Spannung [shpan-∞ng]
Vorsicht! *caution*
Vorsicht, bißiger Hund *beware of the dog*
waist die Taille [tal-yuh]
» *TRAVEL TIP: waist measurements*

UK	24	26	28	30	32	34	36	38
Germany	61	66	71	76	80	87	91	97

wait: will we have to wait long? müssen wir
lange warten? [m∞ssen veer lang-uh varten]
  wait for me warten Sie auf mich [. . . zee ōwf
  mish]
  I'm waiting for a friend ich warte auf einen
  Freund [ish var-tuh ōwf . . .]
waiter der Kellner; **waiter!** (Herr) Ober!
waitress die Kellnerin
  waitress! Fräulein! [froy-line]
wake: will you wake me up at 7.30? wecken
Sie mich, bitte, um 7.30? [vecken zee mish
bittuh ∞m halp ah*k*t]
Wales Wales [v–]
walk: can we walk there? können wir zu Fuß
hingehen? [kurrnen veer tsoo fooss hin-gay-en]
  are there any good walks around here?
  kann man hier gut wandern? [kan man heer
  goot vandern]
  walking shoes die Wanderschuhe [–shoo-uh]
  walking stick der Spazierstock [shpats-*eer*-
  shtock]
wall die Mauer [mōwer]
  (inside) die Wand [vannt]
wallet die Brieftasche [br*eef*-tash-uh]
want: I want a . . . ich möchte ein . . . [ish
murrsh-tuh]
  I want to talk to . . . ich möchte mit . . .
  sprechen

what do you want? was möchten Sie? [vass murrsh-ten zee]

I don't want to ich will nicht [ish vill nisht]

he wants to ... er will ... [air vill]

they don't want to sie wollen nicht

warm warm [varm]

warning die Warnung [varn-oong]

was: I was/he was/it was ich war/er war/es war [... var]

Wartesaal *waiting room*

wash: can you wash these for me? könnten Sie diese für mich waschen? [kurrnt-en zee dee-zuh foor mish vashen]

where can I wash ...? wo kann ich ... waschen? [voh ...]

washing machine die Waschmaschine [vash-mash-een-uh]

washing powder das Waschpulver [–poolver]

washer *(for bolt etc)* die Dichtung [dish-toong]

wasp die Wespe [vesp-uh]

watch: *(wrist-)* die (Armband)uhr [(armbannt)oor]

will you watch ... for me? würden Sie für mich auf ... aufpassen? [voorden zee foor mish oowf ... oowf-pas-en]

watch out! Achtung! [ahk-toong]

water das Wasser [vasser]

can I have some water? kann ich Wasser haben? [kan ish hah-ben]

hot and cold running water fließend kalt und warm Wasser [flee-sent ...]

waterfall der Wasserfall [–fal]

waterproof wasserdicht [–disht]

waterskiing Wasserskilaufen [–shee-lowfen]

way: we'd like to eat the German way wir möchten gerne typisch deutsch essen [veer murrsh-ten gairn-uh toopish doytsh essen]

could you tell me the way to ...? könnten Sie mir den Weg nach ... sagen? [kurrn-ten zee meer dayn vayg nah*k* . . . zah-ghen] *see* **where** *for answers*

we wir [veer]; **we are** wir sind [veer zinnt]

weak schwach [shvah*k*]

weather das Wetter [v–]

   what filthy weather! so ein Hundewetter!
[zoh ine h∞n-duh–]

   what's the weather forecast? was sagt der
Wetterbericht? [vas zahgt dair –buh-risht]

   YOU MAY THEN HEAR . . .

   überwiegend heiter *generally fine*

   leichte/schwere Schauer *light/heavy showers*

   Gewitter *thundery*

   sonnig, warm, kalt *sunny, warm, cold*

Wednesday Mittwoch [mit-vo*k*]

week die Woche [vock-uh]

   a week today/tomorrow heute/morgen in
einer Woche [hoy-tuh/mor-ghen in ine-er . . .]

   at the weekend am Wochenende [am
vock*en*-end-uh]

weight das Gewicht [gheh-v*i*sht]

well: I'm not feeling well ich fühle mich nicht
wohl [ish f∞l-uh mish nisht vole]

   he's not well es geht ihm nicht gut [ess gayt
eem nisht goot]

   how are you? very well, thanks wie geht's?
danke, gut! [vee gayts dankuh goot]

   you speak English very well Sie sprechen
sehr gut Englisch [zee spreshen zair goot
eng-glish]

wellingtons die Gummistiefel [g∞mee-shteefel]

Welsh walisisch [val-*ee*-zish]

   Welshman/-woman Waliser(in)

were: you were Sie waren [zee varen]
(familiar) du warst [doo varst]

   you were *(plural)* Sie waren; *(familiar)* ihr
wart [eer vart] *see* **you**

   we were wir waren [veer . . .]

   they were sie waren

west der Westen [v–]

West Indian westindisch [vest-indish]
(person) Westinder; *(woman)* Westinderin

West Indies die Westindischen Inseln [dee vest-indishen inzeln]

wet naß [nass]

what was [vass]
  what is that? was ist das?
  what for? wozu? [voh-tsoo]
  what room? welches Zimmer? [velshes tsimmer]

wheel das Rad [raht]

when wann [van]; **when I arrived** als ich ankam [alz ish an-kahm]

where wo [voh]
  where is the post office? wo ist das Postamt?
  YOU MAY THEN HEAR . . .
  geradeaus *straight on*
  erste Querstraße links/rechts *first left/right*
  an der Ampel vorbei *past the traffic lights*

which welcher, welche, welches? [velsher . . .]
  which one? welcher?
  YOU MAY THEN HEAR . . .
  dieser, diese, dieses [deezer . . .] *this one*
  der da, die da, das da *that one*
  der, die, das linke *the one on the left*

whisky ein Whisky [v–]

white weiß [vice]

Whitsun Pfingsten

who wer [vair]

wholesale der Großhandel [grohss–]

whose wessen [vessen]
  whose is this? wem gehört das? [vaym gheh-hurrt dass]
  YOU MAY THEN HEAR . . .
  (das gehört) ihm/ihr/mir *(it belongs) to him/her/me*

why warum [varoom]
  why not? warum nicht? [. . . nisht]

wide weit [vite]

wife: my wife meine Frau [mine-uh frōw]

will: when will it be finished? wann ist es fertig? [van isst ess *fairtik*]
  will you do it? tun Sie es? [toon zee ess]

I will come back ich komme wieder [ish kom-uh veeder]

win *(verb)* gewinnen [gheh-vinnen]
 who won? wer hat gewonnen? [vair . . .]

wind *(noun)* der Wind [vinnt]

window das Fenster
 near the window am Fenster

windscreen die Windschutzscheibe [vinnt-shoots-shy-buh]; **windscreeen wipers** die Scheibenwischer [shy-ben-visher]

windy windig [vindi*k*]

wine der Wein [vine]; **can I see the wine list?** kann ich die Getränkekarte haben? [kan ish dee gheh-trenkuh-kartuh h*a*h-ben]

» *TRAVEL TIP: mainly white wines (Weißwein [vice-vine]); fewer reds (Rotwein [roht-vine]); three quality grades* **Tafelwein** *is a table wine without a named vineyard;* **Qualitätswein** *is quality wine from a designated region;* **Qualitätswein mit Prädikat** *is special quality wine; there are countless varieties; some of the main grapes are:* **Riesling** *medium dry;* **Sylvaner** *dry;* **Gutedel** *very dry;* **Müller-Thurgau** *light, fruity;* **Ruländer** *full-bodied, sweetish;* **Traminer** *full-bodied, strong;* **Weißherbst, Schiller** *fruity rosés (Rosé)*

winter der Winter [v–]

wire der Draht; *(elec)* die Leitung [ly-toong]

wish: best wishes alles Gute

with mit

without ohne [oh-nuh]

witness ein Zeuge [tsoy-guh]
 will you act as a witness for me? würden Sie mein Zeuge sein? [v*oo*rden zee mine . . . zine]

woman die Frau [fr*o*w]

women die Frauen [fr*o*wen]

wonderful herrlich [hair-lish]

won't: it won't start es springt nicht an [ess shpringt nisht an]

wood das Holz; *(trees)* der Wald [valt]

wool die Wolle [vol-uh]

word das Wort [vort]
   I don't know that word ich kenne das Wort
   nicht [ish kenn-uh dass . . . nisht]
work *(verb)* arbeiten [ar-by-ten]
   it's not working es funktioniert nicht [ess
   foonk-tsee-oh-n*ee*rt nisht]
   I work in London ich arbeite in London
worry die Sorge [zor-guh]
   I'm worried about him ich mache mir Sorgen
   um ihn [ish mah-*k*uh meer zor-ghen oom een]
   don't worry keine Sorge [kine-uh . . .]
worse: it's worse es ist schlimmer [. . . shl–]
   he's getting worse es geht ihm schlechter [ess
   gayt eem shleshter]
worst schlechteste [shlesht-est-uh]
worth: it's not worth that much so viel ist es
   nicht wert [zoh feel isst ess nisht vairt]
   is it worthwhile going to . . .? lohnt es sich,
   nach . . . zu gehen [. . . zish nah*k* . . . tsoo
   gay-en]
wrap: could you wrap it up? könnten Sie es
   einpacken? [kurrnten zee ess ine–]
wrench *(noun: tool)* der Schraubenschlüssel
   [shr͞owben-shl͞oosel]
wrist das Handgelenk [hannt-gheh–]
write schreiben [shryben]
   could you write it down? könnten Sie das
   aufschreiben? [kurrnten zee dass ͞owf-shryben]
   I'll write to you ich schreibe Ihnen [ish
   shry-buh een-en]
   writing paper das Schreibpapier [shryp-
   papeer]
wrong falsch [falsh]
   I think the bill's wrong ich glaube, die
   Rechnung stimmt nicht [ish gl͞ow-buh dee
   resh-noong shtimmt nisht]
   there's something wrong with . . . da
   stimmt etwas nicht mit . . . [. . . etvass . . .]
   you're wrong Sie irren sich [zee irren zish]
   sorry, wrong number tut mir leid, falsch
   verbunden [toot meer lite falsh fair-boonden]

....

X-ray die Röntgenaufnahme [*ru*rrnt-ghen-ōwf-nah-muh]

yacht die Jacht [yah*k*t]

yard
» *TRAVEL TIP: 1 yard = 91.44 cms = 0.91 m*

year das Jahr [y–]

yellow gelb [ghelp]

yes ja [yah]
   you can't – yes, I can Sie können das nicht – doch! [zee kurrnen dass nisht – do*k*]

yesterday gestern [ghestern]
   the day before yesterday vorgestern [for–]
   yesterday morning/afternoon/evening
   gestern morgen/nachmittag/abend

yet: is it ready yet? ist es fertig? [isst ess *fairtik*]; **not yet** noch nicht [no*k* nisht]

yoghurt ein Joghurt

you Sie [zee]; *(familiar)* du [doo]; *(plural)* Sie [zee]; *(familiar)* ihr [eer]
   I like you ich mag Sie/dich/euch [ish mahg zee/dish/oysh]
   with you mit Ihnen/dir/euch [mit eenen/dir/oysh]
» *TRAVEL TIP: use the 'Sie' forms in most situations; the 'du' forms are for people you know well*

young jung [yo͝ong]

your Ihr [eer]; *(familiar)* dein [dine] *(plural)* euer [oy-er]
   is this yours? ist es Ihrer/deiner?

youth hostel die Jugendherberge [yoo-ghent-hair-bair-guh]
» *TRAVEL TIP: only Bavaria has an age limit of 27*

zero Null [no͝ol]
   below zero unter Null [o͝onter . . .]

ziehen *pull*

Zimmer frei *vacancies, rooms*

zip der Reißverschluß [*r*ice-fair-shlo͝oss]

Zoll *Customs*

Zutritt verboten *no admission*

zu verkaufen *for sale*

zu vermieten *for hire/to let*

0 null [nool]
1 eins [ine-ts]
2 zwei [tsvy]
3 drei [dry]
4 vier [feer]
5 fünf [foonf]
6 sechs [zex]
7 sieben [zeeben]
8 acht [ah*k*t]
9 neun [noyn]
10 zehn [tsayn]
11 elf
12 zwölf [tsvurrlf]
13 dreizehn [dry-tsayn]
14 vierzehn
15 fünfzehn
16 sechzehn
40 vierzig
50 fünfzig
60 sechzig
100 hundert [hoondert]
175 hundertfünfundsiebzig
    [hoondert-foonf-oont-zeep-tsi*k*]
200 zweihundert
1,000 tausend [tow-zent]
2,000 zweitausend
1,000,000 eine Million [ine-uh mil-ee-yone]

17 siebzehn [zeep–]
18 achtzehn
19 neunzehn
20 zwanzig
    [tsvan-tsi*k*]
21 einundzwanzig
    [ine-oont–]
22 zweiundzwanzig
23 dreiundzwanzig
24 vierundzwanzig
25 fünfundzwanzig
26 sechsundzwanzig
27 siebenundzwanzig
28 achtundzwanzig
29 neunundzwanzig
30 dreißig [dry-si*k*]
31 einunddreißig
70 siebzig [zeep–]
80 achtzig
90 neunzig
101 hunderteins

*NB: the German comma is a decimal point; for
thousands use a full-stop, eg 2.000*

The German alphabet
a [ah] *b* [bay] *c* [tsay] *d* [day] *e* [ay] *f* [eff]
g [gay] *h* [hah] *i* [ee] *j* [yot] *k* [kah] *l* [el]
m [em] *n* [en] *o* [oh] *p* [pay] *q* [koo] *r* [air]
s [ess] *t* [tay] *u* [oo] *v* [fow] *w* [vay] *x* [eeks]
y [oop-zee-lon] *z* [tset] *ß* = ss